From
CLAY *to* KILN

From
CLAY *to* KILN

A BEGINNER'S GUIDE TO THE POTTER'S WHEEL

STUART CAREY

PHOTOGRAPHY BY ALUN CALLENDER

LARK
New York

New York

An Imprint of Sterling Publishing Co., Inc.
1166 Avenue of the Americas
New York, NY 10036

© 2019 Quarto Publishing PLC
An imprint of The Quarto Group

ISBN 978-1-4547-1092-9

Distributed in Canada by Sterling
Publishing Co., Inc.
c/o Canadian Manda Group, 664
Annette Street
Toronto, Ontario M6S 2C8, Canada

For information about custom
editions, special sales, and premium
and corporate purchases, please
contact Sterling Special Sales
at 800-805-5489 or
specialsales@sterlingpublishing.com.

Manufactured in China

2 4 6 8 10 9 7 5 3 1

sterlingpublishing.com
larkcrafts.com

Photography by Alun Callender

MIX
Paper from
responsible sources
FSC® C016973

CONTENTS

MEET STUART

I'm Stuart, and I am a contemporary ceramics maker from Newcastle upon Tyne in the UK. I threw my first pot when I was fourteen in all-too-rare school pottery classes under the guidance of my mentor and friend Glyn Thomas. I say I threw a pot, but it was more like a round lump with a hole in the middle. (I think my mam still has it, but it's probably more useful as a door stop than a vessel.) Despite the primitive outcome, I could see the potential and knew with persistence and passion I had found a creative outlet that sung to me in a way I'd never felt before. I was hooked.

What I love about clay is its possibility—especially in today's society where we are rarely so free. Even when designing using the most modern of computer programs, we're still working within a set of contrived parameters. Clay has its own limits, of course, but to be faced with a shapeless lump and mold it how you like is true freedom to me. It's a relationship. Clay "talks" to you. As much as you try to control it, you have to strike up a partnership and understanding to get what you want out of it.

Now, I am a professional ceramicist, teacher, and writer. I've taught at Central Saint Martins and lectured at the Royal College of Art and, today, I co-run The Kiln Rooms, one of London's most popular open-access ceramics studios for all-skill level students. The Kiln Rooms give me a unique insight into the problems that newcomers face when working with this intuitively physical material.

My signature style is delicate, elegant forms, derived from design training but steeped in the history of ceramics and a love for the material. I've always had a passion for tableware as I enjoy the interaction between user and object. I strive to make work that feels and functions as good as it looks and makes its audience want to interact with it.

In this book, I give insights into how I handle clay, from hand building to throwing on my beloved wheel, and on through to glazing and decorating. I give tips, tricks, and recipes honed over the past seventeen years, some "borrowed" from my master tutors, such as Emmanuel Cooper and Takeshi Yasuda, but most developed through my determination to achieve both elegance and efficiency in production.

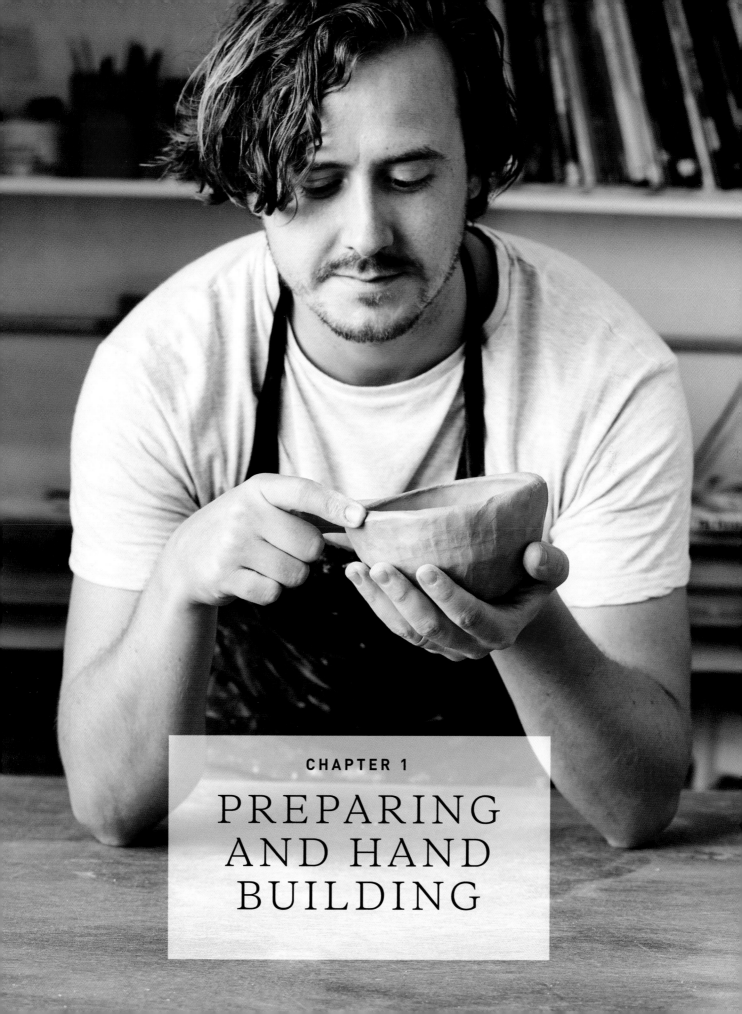

CHAPTER 1

PREPARING AND HAND BUILDING

MEET THE MATERIALS

Commercial clays come in many colors and textures, and all you have to do is order them online. Gone are the days of digging for your own clay. Although there is something romantic about doing this, buying the clay is easier. With the processing time saved and less land available for digging, this option is also cheaper. The selection of clays is vast, and you may be wondering where to begin. Deciding what you would like to make is a great starting point.

In general, clay comes in three types: earthenware, stoneware, and porcelain. There are lots of variations within these types, but all clays can usually be placed in one of these categories. The biggest difference among the types is the firing temperature. Earthenware has a low standard firing temperature for tableware of 1,940-2,156°F (1,060-1,180°C); stoneware is 2,192-2,372°F (1,200-1,300°C); and porcelain is 2,228-2,462°F (1,220-1,350°C), although there are exceptions. Lower-temperature earthenware clays and glazes tend to be a bit softer once fired, and are slightly prone to chipping and breakage as a result. They do, however, have the least breakages in the kiln, as lower firing temperatures present fewer risks. They're also good for bright solid colors. Stoneware clays are a bit more durable and just as easy to work with. There's a bit more risk of breakages in the kiln, but the higher temperature opens up a world of glaze possibilities. Porcelain is the lightest in color and possibly the most beautiful surface for glaze. The clay is very fine and probably the most difficult to master. It is also prone to warping at very high temperatures.

I have chosen to work with a fine white stoneware in my own practice.

I find it is best for constructing forms on a wheel, without too much grit, and I can achieve fine delicate works with a body that is light enough to show off the glaze and a firing range that allows for a soft, organic palette.

For the purposes of this book, I will be using this white stoneware for all the projects. We will limit our exploration to that firing range. Although this eliminates earthenware and some porcelains, which have just as much value, I feel their discussion would be better left for another time.

Let's take a look at some clays in the 2,192-2,372°F (1,200-1,300°C) firing range that I have worked with and stock in my studios.

1 WHITE SPECIAL STONEWARE
A light-firing fine clay. Not too gritty, but strong enough for large, thin items and hand building. The body takes glaze well, and it's fairly robust in the firing process. Darker or flecked versions are also available and are known as buff. They provide a darker canvas for glaze, and small iron spots often appear throughout the surface.

2 CRANK
A highly grogged (see Glossary, page 155), toasty firing clay. This additive gives the clay lots of strength, but can leave the body

"open," which means it requires a glaze to make it watertight. It can be used in a 50/50 combination with any of the other fine clays described here to change its color, make a strong but less gritty clay, and help with vitrification (watertightness).

3 VULCAN BLACK FINE
A very smooth, black firing clay that is good for throwing and fine ware. The high oxide content, which gives it its color, can make glazes react during firing, causing bubbling, blistering, and pinholing. However, it also creates very pleasing results when paired with white glazes.

4 VULCAN BLACK GROGGED
As above, but with more of the consistency of crank. As opposed to mixing crank and vulcan black fine, this clay has strength and texture while retaining its dark color.

5 DL PORCELAIN
A porcelain with a stoneware firing range (by David Leach). This forgiving porcelain works well as a throwing body. As with all porcelain, it can be a little unforgiving for hand building but is my choice when required. It is a slightly creamy white and has fair translucency when thin. It takes glaze well, but encourages crazing (see Glossary, page 154) with stoneware gloss glazes.

WEDGING

Wedging is the process of mixing and de-airing clay. While there are many variations in hand position and technique, here I demonstrate two common methods and hand positions that have served me well and provide reliable results. Wedging is also often referred to as kneading, because of its similarity to kneading dough. There is one big difference: in baking, you fold air into the mix, but we use the process to do the opposite in ceramics. But don't worry about the language, just let your hands do the talking!

LEFT Here I'm wedging 11 pounds (5 kg) of clay. I'll then cut it into ten balls to make 18-ounce (500 g) pasta bowls.

BOAR'S SKULL WEDGING

This technique is known by many names, including bull's nose and ram's head, descriptions that are all derived from the shape the clay takes during the wedging process. The basic principle is to stretch and compress layers of clay, working with a whole lump and repeating the process over and over. Over time, you will start to feel a slight but noticeable resistance from the clay when it is fully wedged. This moment signifies the clay has been properly compressed. Until you're familiar with how this feels, a good rule of thumb is to repeat the following steps fifty times, regardless of the size of the ball of clay.

1 Begin with a roughly round ball and place your hands on top, as shown. Begin applying pressure downward, from the heel of your thumbs and palm, while using the middle of your palms and the base of your other fingers to contain the clay and stop it from spreading out.

2 Push down and slightly forward into the clay, ensuring you indent the clay. Take care not to push too hard, or you'll create indents that will trap air in the next step. This process is much more about repetition and the accurate execution of the process than the strength used. Be careful not to trap your fingers under the ball—instead, allow them to spread as they meet the work surface.

1

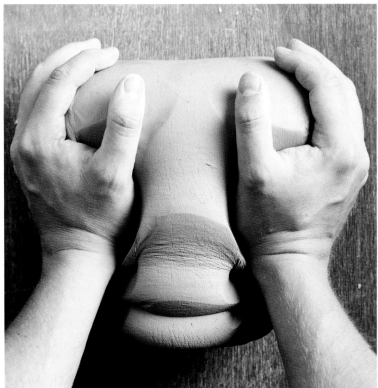

2

3 Rock the ball back, right up onto its "nose," then move your hands back to the top of the ball. Repeat this movement, ensuring you don't "fold" the clay. You are trying to compress the clay from the top and stretch a layer across the bottom in order to pop any air bubbles.

4 You'll be able to see the layers forming at the "mouth." I like to call these smiles (4a). Repeat steps 1–4 fifty times. As you get to the end of the fifty repetitions, reduce the pressure with each push until you are rolling the clay into a nice round form. Drop and roll the clay onto its ends to round off the creased sides. Slap the creases out of the ends and pat the "head" into a longer "sausage" shape that is ready for cutting, weighing, and balling. Once you've finished, you can cut the ball in half to check for air bubbles, and start again if you find any (4b).

NOTE At first, as you learn how to wedge clay, the process will seem disjointed, but, as you get more comfortable with it, the action will become fluid: contain the clay with your cupped hands, push down and spread your fingers, lift the clay back with a flick of the fingers, and then catch the clay again with the heel of your thumb.

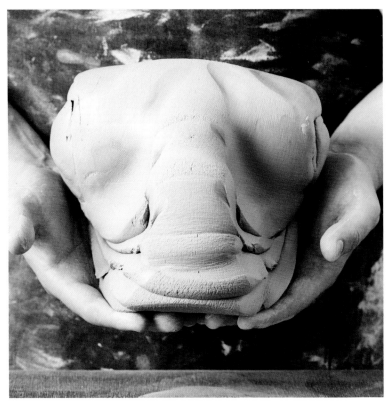

4a

4b

CUT AND SLAM

Although this technique is very different from Boar's Skull Wedging (see pages 13-15), it works according to the same principles. This method produces visible layers and can be satisfying when you're mixing clays of different colors, as you can see the process in action. Here you cut a lump of clay in half (see Cutting, page 19) and slam the two halves back together, stacking the layers on top of each other. The layers double with each repetition. A short boar's skull wedge can finish the clay off nicely for weighing and balling (see page 19).

1 Begin with a squared-off lump of clay. I am using two different colors—white stoneware and vulcan black grogged. Hold the clay at one end and drop it on the table, so you can shape it and get a wire under the half facing you without cutting into the clay. Pull the wire up through the clay, parallel to your body (as shown).

2 Lift one piece and turn it upside down so that the two cut edges are facing in the same direction. Slam the lifted piece down onto the piece on the table. When you slam the top piece down, you need to start from the edge of one end first. This stops air from getting trapped between the layers. To check if you have done this correctly, listen to the sound the clay makes: if you hear a slap, you've probably trapped some air; if the slam sounds duller, you've avoided this.

3 Pick up the whole lump and flip it over away from you. Slam it onto the table to compress it back into the original shape. Lift the clay off the table again and rotate it (don't roll it) a quarter turn (this can be to the right or left, but use the same direction each time). This helps to mix the clay, so you cut it from a different side every time. Place the clay back down as in step 1, and repeat.

4 Repeat steps 1–3 thirty to forty times—by this time, the layers should be blended beyond visible difference. Each time you repeat the process, you double the number of layers, effectively squaring the number of repetitions. So by 40 repetitions, you have 1,600 layers. This action is also good for mixing firm and softer clays (within reason). To finish, knead lightly, ball up the clay, and cut to size.

LEFT A cross section of cut-and-slam wedging showing the layering effect.

1

2

3

4

WEIGHING AND BALLING

Weighing and balling is an important preparation stage that is often overlooked in the novice potter's impatience with starting a project.

Weighing is useful because it helps minimize trimmings and waste. It ensures that you know how much you can achieve from a specific ball of clay, and sets the parameters for what's possible before you start. It's also a great way to test your skill and mark your progress. A good exercise for throwing, for example, is to throw a cylinder every day from the same weight of clay. You'll find you can make larger and larger pieces, and develop the skills needed to use all the clay.

Balling is simply the process of making the clay round before you use it. This is required in most cases, but if you don't intend to make something round, the shape may not be essential.

Using a patted-out "sausage" shape of wedged clay, I like to estimate the size of the piece I need and then cut one piece at a time to weigh. Once the piece of clay is on the scale, I add a little or cut some off until I'm within a gram or two of my desired weight. Your accuracy may vary depending on how important the weight is, but every gram counts when you are throwing fine ware.

Ball the clay by patting it into a round shape with a cupped hand. If there are creases on the surface, slap them out with the flat of your fingers. A slapping sound here is good. I always encourage students to start with a crease-free ball. Maybe I'm a bit of a perfectionist, but it just feels better to start with a blank clay canvas.

CUTTING

Cutting clay is a fairly simple process. The best tool to use is a wire (see Tools, page 47), which works like a cheese wire. Holding an end of the wire in each hand, stretch it taut, then simply pull it through the clay where you want it cut. I prefer working with a twisted wire, but there are many types of wire for many different jobs.

HAND
BUILDING

Hand building is an ancient pottery-making technique that involves the creation of forms without a pottery wheel, using only the hands, fingers, and simple tools. My favorite hand-building techniques are pinching, coiling, and press molding.

PINCHING

Pinching is a very useful skill, and you can learn a huge amount about clay from this simple technique. A pinch pot is a clay vessel that's formed with the hands only. As the name suggests, it is the action of pinching the clay between the fingers and thumb that molds the clay and spreads out the surface area to form an object. For me, the beauty of pinch pots lies in the primitive physical engagement of hand and clay: your brain is learning from the sense of touch and aligning that with what you see. This interaction creates tacit knowledge or muscle memory, and is vital in understanding how to manipulate clay successfully. By making several pinch pots you will learn how much pressure you can apply, how far clay can stretch, when to use water, when to compress, how thin is too thin, and much more. All these skills are transferable to all aspects of ceramic production.

Here, we are going to make a cereal-sized bowl from 18 ounces (500 g) of clay. As I'm right-handed, I will explain the following from my perspective; if you are left-handed, you may want to reverse the hands.

1 Begin with a ball of clay suitable for the size of the bowl you'd like to make. With the right thumb, press into the center of the ball against the opposite palm and press from the outside with your right fingers. With your right hand, use a small pinch, a short rotation (only a few millimeters), and gentle pressure. The less pressure you use and the shorter the turn, the more even the bowl will be.

2 Gradually push your thumb down into the base of the clay. Start pinching the wall of the pot from the bottom, constantly rotating a few millimeters with every pinch. As you squeeze the clay, it will become wider and force the form outward.

3 Continue turning and pinching, working your way up the wall of the bowl, thinning the clay out gently. The bowl will begin to open up.

1

2

3

4

5

4 As you approach the rim, you may find that the clay looks as if it's beginning to crack around the lip. Before this becomes a problem, compress the clay by rubbing it down with your finger—you will need to repeat this as the rim gets wider and wider.

Stop pinching before the bowl is as wide as you'd like, because it's much easier to push the shape out than it is to bring it back in. Try to get a consistent thickness in the walls all the way around.

Shape the bowl using gentle pinches. At this stage you may also want to use a curved kidney tool (see page 48) to shape the inside of the bowl.

5 You can allow the bowl to firm up and work on the surfaces with a metal kidney to achieve a completely smooth appearance. However, I prefer the integrity of a pinch pot that retains the marks of the maker, so I've just refined the surface a little with my fingers and a rubber kidney but allowed some of the making marks to show through. Run a sponge around the rim to soften and smooth the edge, which makes all the difference to the finishing.

COILING

Coiling is the process of building pots layer by layer, normally using round lengths of clay. The beauty of coil pots lies in their versatility of size and shape. A coil pot can take on any form and is not solely limited to the round. It also provides a chance to work on a scale that can be limited by the wheel or press-mold. The action of building one layer at a time offers an opportunity to consider the form at all stages.

You can make coils by rolling, squeezing, or extruding. Here, we are going to use round extruded coils, approximately ½ inch (12 mm) wide, cut to length depending on the needs of the pot. The process of extruding requires a piece of equipment known as an extruder or wad box. These come in all shapes and sizes, ranging from handheld to wall-mounted or freestanding, but all work on the same principle. Clay is compressed and squeezed through a cutout profile of the shape and size required to create a length of clay. If you want to see more examples, have a look at the section on handles, pages 116–119.

When coiling, it's useful to make batches of long coils (the length of your arm is a good guide for the size). Store the coils wrapped in plastic, so they don't dry out.

Keep a bowl handy for scraps. If you don't let them dry out, they can be wedged and reused. If they do dry out, they tend to be very easy to rehydrate because of their size. Working on a banding wheel (aka whirler) can be very useful because you can turn the pot with ease. If you want a thin base, be sure to put a cloth or some newspaper between the base and the wheel head; otherwise it will need wiring off if it sticks.

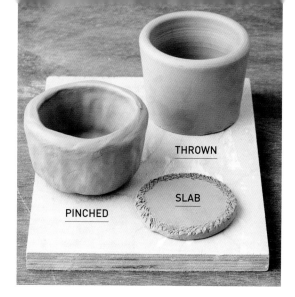

THROWN

PINCHED

SLAB

There are three ways to make the base to start a coil pot. You can use a rolled-out slab, or pinch or throw a small pot. When working on a slab, cut the slab to size, then score and slip the top edge of the slab and the bottom side of the first coil—as you would when attaching a handle (see Handles, pages 116–119). Add the coil as shown in step 2 and apply pressure downward all the way around to secure the coil in place. Take off any excess slip that has squeezed out of the edges and join the coil. This can be a little messy, but it is just for the first coil and worth doing to attach the base fully. For a pinched or thrown base, make the pot as thick as the coils you're using. There is no need to score and slip the edge, but ideally, it should be left smooth and curved to mirror the coil coming down on top. I use a thrown base to start.

1 Before starting, draw and cut out the shape you intend to create to scale. A working drawing is always useful, and if you are creating a shape on the round, you can use the outside of the drawing as a profile (see Glossary, page 155). This can be a great way to keep the form within the intended perimeters. When working to a profile, try to keep the pot slightly inside the shape, as it's easy to push out the shape at the later stages, but very difficult to bring it back in.

2 To add a coil, wrap a length of clay above the previous layer, be it another coil, the rim of a pot, or a flat base. Overlap and cut through the ends. Remove the short tail (the shorter the better for less waste).

1

2

3

4

5

6

3 Lift the two ends and push them together from the bottom to avoid trapping air. Rub over the join with your finger to seal it well.

4 With one finger or a thumb, work the coil from the middle, pressing downward to attach it to the clay below. Work all the way around, on the outside first, then on the inside. The surface may look quite rough, but don't worry too much about that at this stage. Just be sure the coils are well joined. You may have noticed that the coil has thinned out by about half. This is fine because when you add the next coil and work it down, it will thicken the first coil, and so on. Continue this

process. If the pot starts to feel a bit wobbly or saggy, you can firm it up a little with a blow-dryer. Avoid drying out the top, however, as this needs to be soft to take the next coil.

5 To bring the form in or out, simply place the coil a little on the inside or outside of the pot. This will help you to follow your profile.

6 For roughly every 6 inches (15 cm) you gain in height, take some time to work the surface. This can largely be done by hand or, where you feel it's relevant, with a wooden or metal kidney. Try not to sponge or dampen the surface.

7a

7b

8a

8b

7 Once you have reached the desired height, and the pot is sitting a little within your desired profile (7a), begin shaping and refining. A gentle push from the inside can stretch the walls out to the desired form—a gradual approach is advisable (7b).

8 Use a metal kidney to scrape off any excess clay and a wooden one to help blend the surface. This will help seal up all the joins (8a). You can also burnish the surface with the back of a spoon or something with a similar surface—use a gentle, circular action, working on an area about the size of a penny (UK 2-pence) with each repetition (8b). This action creates a nice surface and also compresses the clay, making the form very strong and less likely to fracture along a coil join. Finish with a rubber kidney.

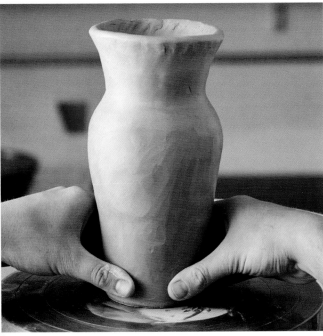

9

10

9 If you are reasonably proficient with a potter's wheel and you are working on the round, you may want to spend some time finishing on the wheel. Apply a tiny drop of water to the wheel head and smear this around to create a sticky surface. Place the pot firmly on the wheel head and move it around a little until you feel the moisture grabbing the base. Push the pot as close to the center as possible—you may want to look at the section on Turning (see pages 95–96) for tips on centering a pot.

10 Cautiously, as it is possible for the pot to release unexpectedly, trim excess clay away with turning tools and throw the neck of the piece using as little water as possible. Trim the lip and thin it out. This provides an opportunity to refine the pot to a perfectly round form.

PRESS MOLDING

Press molding is a very useful way of making repeated forms. Molds are available in all shapes, sizes, and styles. There's more than enough for a whole book on the subject, so here we're keeping it simple and working just with a plate mold. The mold I use here is made of plaster and was designed for use on a machine, but it works perfectly well when working by hand. Molds are usually made of plaster because it is a very fine material capable of capturing the smallest of details. Plaster is also fairly strong once it has set, meaning that the mold can be used hundreds of times if it is well looked after. The molds are very absorbent, which means they dry out the clay. This is very useful because, as the clay dries, it shrinks, lifting itself from the mold. The piece is then easily turned out for drying and the mold is ready to be used again. It's advisable to keep molds in a dry environment and give them some time to dry between uses, although for press molding they can often be used two or three times before the clay starts to stick. Always start with a clean, dust-free mold.

LEFT Plaster press molds of varying styles with tools, clay, and plates at different stages.

RIGHT Weighing and preparing slabs for press molding. Here the slabs are rolled by hand using a rolling pin on a cloth.

1 Begin by rolling out a slab of wedged clay. Make sure to have enough clay—it is better to have too much than too little. It's also best to beat the clay as flat as possible before rolling. This will save lots of time and effort. Here, we're rolling by hand using two ¼-inch (6 mm) sticks as guides, to stop the clay from getting any thinner and to get consistent thickness. I use a cut-up acrylic shower curtain liner as a rolling cloth because it's thin, light, and dries quickly. The weave is also very small, so it doesn't add texture to the clay and tends not to crease under the clay either. A dish towel or canvas cloth are also fine, but having tried lots of different materials, I find this to be a cheap and useful option. I turn the clay regularly while rolling to avoid directional marks and to prevent warping.

1
—

RIGHT You can also use a slab roller to roll out the clay. These come in all shapes and sizes, but the principles are the same as for rolling by hand. I suggest setting the slab roller to roll a little thicker than you need and gradually get thinner while rotating the clay and rerolling until you reach the required thickness three or four times.

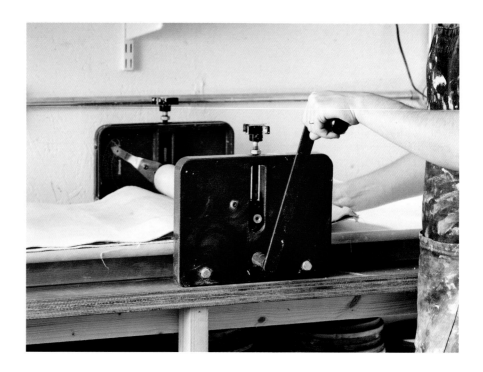

2

3

2 Keep the slab on your rolling cloth and clean the surface facing you with a rubber kidney. This is the surface that will be pressed against the mold and, as a result, there won't be much opportunity to work on this surface later as it will be fairly dry when it comes out of the mold. As such, it's important that this surface looks smooth before you use the piece of clay.

3 Lift the slab from under the rolling cloth and turn it upside down, draping it into the mold as you would a piecrust in a pie plate. Remove the cloth from the surface. Placing the mold on a banding wheel can be useful at this stage. Gently press from the center of the plate outward, so that the slab takes the form of the mold and any air under the clay is pushed out.

4 At this stage, I've found it helpful to slap the clay against the mold while slowly rotating. This ensures the outside of the form takes to the shape of the mold. It also compresses the clay firmly into the shape, meaning it shouldn't warp in the heat of the kiln.

4

5

6

7

5 Cut the excess clay from the rim using a wire. Here, I'm using a one-handed wire known as a bow harp.

6 Using a sharp plastic or wooden tool with a flat edge, scrape away any excess clay from the rim. Always cut toward the mold edge to avoid pulling the clay away from the form. Try not to use metal tools on plaster, as they can easily scratch and spoil your mold.

7 This particular plate has a foot ring. For a plate with a flat base, skip to step 9. Here, the ring needs to be filled from the inside to create a flat interior. It's always best to fill from the inside, as this area is more accessible for working. Rub down the inside of the foot ring to create a smooth surface and dampen this very slightly. Roll out a thick coil and add it to the ring groove, pushing firmly downward all the way around.

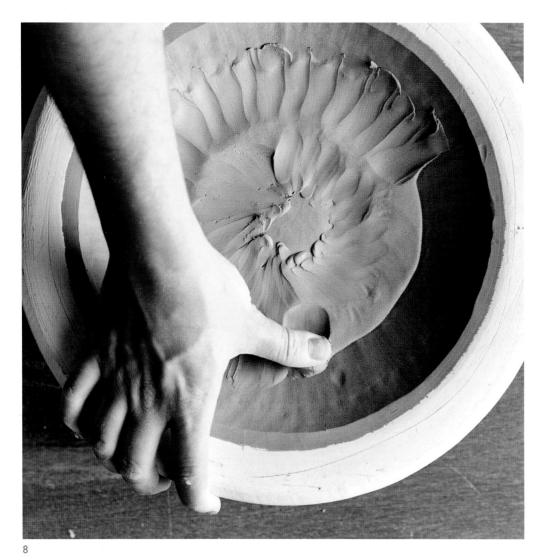

8

9

8 Work the coil into the plate on the inside and outside, by pushing from the center with your thumb.

9 Spend some time working the surface, using a wooden kidney to move the clay and a metal one to remove any excess. With some practice, this process can allow you to create a beautifully smooth surface. Consider how you want to finish the rim. Here, I've thinned it out to a fine point where it meets the mold, in order to give a delicate look to the plate once it's removed. If your mold will fit on a potter's wheel, you can also do a little finishing with a damp sponge. You can "fake in" throwing rings or use it for decorative purposes.

10

10 Let the plate dry in the mold (this could take anywhere from an hour to a day depending on the environment). Once the clay has shrunk away from the edge of the mold all the way around the rim, lift the mold, placing one hand in the middle of the clay surface and holding the other one under the mold. Flip the mold over, keeping one hand underneath and using your other hand to press the mold against your body. This will allow you to release the plate from the underside (see opposite). Releasing the plate can be a bit of a juggling act, so be careful. Where possible, get someone to help you when using larger molds.

11 Once the plate is out of the mold, run a slightly damp sponge around the rim to soften the edge. Check the underside for faults, sponge where necessary, and let dry.

RIGHT Turning out a plate from the mold as described in step 10.

11

CHAPTER 2

THROWING

BODY POSITION

When working any physical job, you need to protect yourself from short- and long-term injury. Here is a set of simple rules and stretches to prolong your working career and cut down on time taken off due to injury.

Having your body in the right position for throwing for any length of time is crucial to prevent chronic pain and, in some cases, severe repetitive injury. When seated, always keep your heel in front of your knee and your knee lower than your hip—this position allows the blood to flow more easily and helps prevent cramping and aching knees and hips. Tilt your stool forward so you do not have to lean over as much. You can get an adjustable stool or simply prop up the back legs with boards. Keep your back as straight as possible. You can raise up the wheel on bricks or boards to suit your position. Wheel leg extenders are also available. I suggest putting your non-action foot on boards to mirror the height of your pedal foot. This will keep your spine straight.

Place a mirror behind the wheel, so that you can see the profile of the pot without bending over. This regular twisting action is one of the main causes of back pain. Keep your shoulders low at all times and try not to bunch them up. Use your body weight by leaning into the clay during centering rather than pushing with your strength. Wedge your elbows into your body or thighs where possible to keep you steady and increase your strength without having to use muscles.

TIP Potters are forever picking up heavy bags of clay, pails of glaze, dry materials, and kiln shelves. Keeping these on the floor makes sense, but this increases the distance to lift. When lifting, keep your back straight, bend at the knees, securely hold the weight, and lift with your legs. This will avoid sudden trauma, twisted or pulled muscles, or lumbar impact.

LEFT Sit at the wheel with a raised stool and legs on the wheel.

STRETCHES

The following are three very quick and useful stretches recommended to me by an osteopath. I have found them very useful in preventing recurring back pain. However, if any of this feels uncomfortable, I suggest you seek professional advice. I do these stretches every morning and also regularly while working. The idea is to open up the muscles opposite to those you use while working—this keeps you balanced and not overworked in one direction and should help with upper and lower back pain.

1 Place your hands in front of you in a praying position. Interlace your fingers together, leaving the thumbs and index fingers pointed like a gun. Raise your hands up to the ceiling, as if you're reaching to touch it with your index fingers. Relax your rib cage and lean over to your left until you feel the right-hand side of your chest stretch. Hold for five seconds, gently release, and repeat, this time leaning to the right. Keep your ribs low and stretch as much as you can with your pointed hands.

2 Place your hands together behind your back and make a gun shape with the index fingers pointing toward the ground. Keeping yourself straight and upright, lower your hands down as if you're trying to touch the floor. Feel the stretch in your shoulders and hold for five seconds. Keeping your hands stretched, gently roll your head back and from side to side. Feel the pull in your upper chest, repeat for 5–10 seconds, and gently release.

3 Stand in front of an open doorway and place your hands and forearms on each side of the frame at chest height. Be sure of your footing, then lean forward through the door frame, keeping your shoulders low. Feel the stretch in your pectorals. Hold for five seconds and carefully move back to standing. Repeat two or three times.

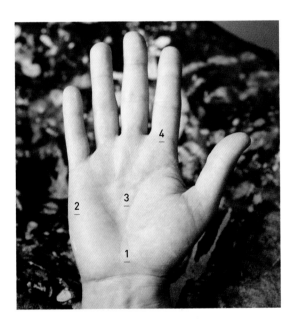

THE HAND

While we call on specialized tools in pottery processes to produce specific results, there is very little that can't be done by hand alone. In throwing, in particular, potters tend to work up the hand from the strongest parts to weakest, as the clay requires a more delicate touch in the later stages. As we work up the hand, we find our sensitivity increases, giving us a fantastic insight into how the clay is doing under the strains of production and a warning when we're close to disaster. It takes years to train and understand your hands, but with lots of practice they can tell you more than you can see with the eye.

1 Heel The heel is the strongest part of the hand. It is a blunt end that channels the strength of your entire arm. When your elbow is locked into your thigh or waist, you can push your body weight straight through, making it a perfect tool for power and strength. The heel is the least sensitive, as it has a broad surface, and is used to move lots of clay.

2 Side The side of your palm when the fist is clenched can be a very strong mover of clay. By locking your arm, or even placing your other hand on top, you can create immense downward pressure with your body weight. This is great for moving lots of clay when you're working on large pieces or wide dishes and plates.

3 Palm The palm and the base of your fingers make good containers—they are strong but sensitive enough to relay information on how far the clay is moving and at what speed. These areas are particularly useful when you are centering.

4 Fingers The broad width of the index finger can be used for multiple tasks: held straight, it acts like a rib; curled tight, it offers a broad lifting hook. The fingertips have the most sensitivity, which is vital in the later stages of creating a pot. They can sense how soft, wet, or thin the clay has become and let you know where to push more and where to leave well alone. Though there isn't much natural strength in your fingertips, they are vital for shaping and finishing—good control can be the difference between clunky and considered.

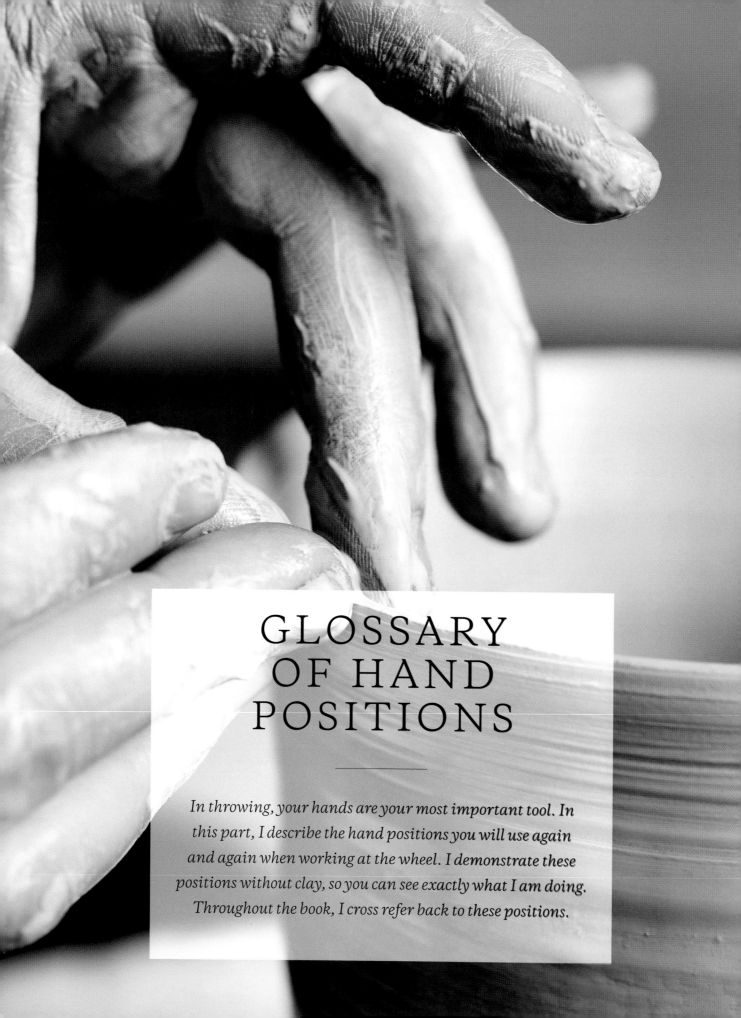

GLOSSARY OF HAND POSITIONS

In throwing, your hands are your most important tool. In this part, I describe the hand positions you will use again and again when working at the wheel. I demonstrate these positions without clay, so you can see exactly what I am doing. Throughout the book, I cross refer back to these positions.

1

1. HOOK AND ANCHOR

Use the heel of your left hand as a firm anchor by lodging your elbow into your hip. This will serve as a profile that holds the clay in a round form. Create a hook with your right hand and place it at the back of the clay. From the base of your fingers, pull the clay back toward the anchor—this squeezing motion brings the clay upward into a cone shape. Don't try to lift the clay, as the inward squeeze forces it up. To bring the clay back down, raise your right hand so that the center of the palm sits on the top right corner of the clay, then push over and down into the anchor, making sure to hold the left hand steady.

2

2. PINT GLASS

Hold the side of the clay in your left hand, as if it were a pint glass. Be careful not to squeeze inward with your thumb. This is a supporting position and not an action position.

3

3. KARATE CHOP

Maintaining stability by resting on the "pint glass" left hand, form a chopping shape with your right hand and hold in place to compress and flatten the clay.

4

4. CUB SCOUTS

Straighten the index and middle finger of your right hand, as if giving a "Scout's honor" salute. Resting on the "pint glass" formed by your left hand, keep the salute straight and apply pressure with the pads of the fingertips (not the actual tips). The ends of the fingers will bend back slightly against the pressure on the clay. This creates compression rather than a cutting action.

5

5. THUMBS UP

We rarely use two hands opposite each other on the outside of the pot like this. However, this hand position is useful in the early stages to bring the base in to the desired width. Simply hold your hands straight vertically and gently squeeze inward until your piece is the required internal width (see Cylinder, step 4, page 61).

6

6. CRAB CLAW

Hold the wall of the clay with a pincer-like left hand, ensuring that the thumb on the outside is opposite the index finger on the inside. Place your hand on the right-hand side of the pot at between the 4 and 5 o'clock positions.

7. TRIGGER FINGER

Stick out your right hand like a gun, with the thumb raised and index finger pointing out. Then pull the trigger and keep the index finger bent at the end (with only two bent knuckles). Now twist your hand so your thumb is pointing to the left. Keeping the shape tight, drop your fingers down toward the floor so your thumbnail goes from facing your body to facing the ceiling.

7

8. CRAB CLAW AND TRIGGER FINGER

Bring the two hand positions together by placing the right thumb on the hand knuckle of the left index finger. Place the tip of the right index finger (with the nail side facing down) against the left side of the left thumb tip. Allow the right index finger to push the left thumb back slightly, so it is now directly opposite the left index fingertip. The wall of the pot is squeezed between these two points and supported by the other fingers.

8

9. TIP TO TIP

Squeeze the wall of the pot gently between the middle fingertips, with the left hand on the inside and the right hand on the outside, working at a point between the 4 and 5 o'clock positions. The middle fingers are supported by at least one finger on each side, and the inside hand sits very slightly above the outside one, leading the movement.

9

10

10. TIP TO RIB

Using the same position for the left hand as Tip to Tip (see page 43), use a rib on the outside to compress, straighten, and clean the outside of the pot. For lifting and cleaning, let the clay slide off the rib by angling it away from you. For cutting or trimming, hold the rib straight against the side of the pot.

11

11. EDGE FINGERS

This position compresses the rim during throwing and leaves a smooth edge on the vessel. Hold the rim gently between the index finger and thumb of the left hand, then hold a sponge to the rib in the right hand and gently compress.

12

12. TRIANGLE HANDS

This hand position is for the process known as collaring, which turns a wide form into a narrower one. Form a triangle with your hands. Start with the index fingers and thumbs at the base of the pot, then add in fingers as you draw your hands slowly upward. You must use slow hands with a medium to quick wheel speed here.

13. THE PULL BACK

Position your left hand in a "pint-glass" position (see page 41) and place it at the 6 o'clock position. Use the curve between your thumb and index finger as a rest for a "cub scouts" position with your right hand. Turn the "cub scouts" hand down so that your fingertips are touching the base of the interior, and pull both hands as one unit back toward you to open up the pot.

13

14. FIST PRESS

Cup the clay with the side of your left hand to support the clay from the outside and stop it flaring out too quickly. For plates and wide, shallow forms, use the side heel of your right hand. First compress the centered clay downward and then pull back toward yourself to open the clay out. The idea is to squash the clay flat across the wheel head rather than rolling it outward. Use the left hand to support the outer edge. Where possible, it will help if you can place a thumb between your hands for extra stability.

14

15. BACK-HANDED KIDNEY

For shaping and cleaning the inside of bowls and plates, use a kidney tool held in the right hand against the left-hand-side interior of the pot. This position gives you more dexterity in the wrist than working on the right-hand side. The tip of the kidney should be facing slightly toward you, to allow the clay to slide off it.

15

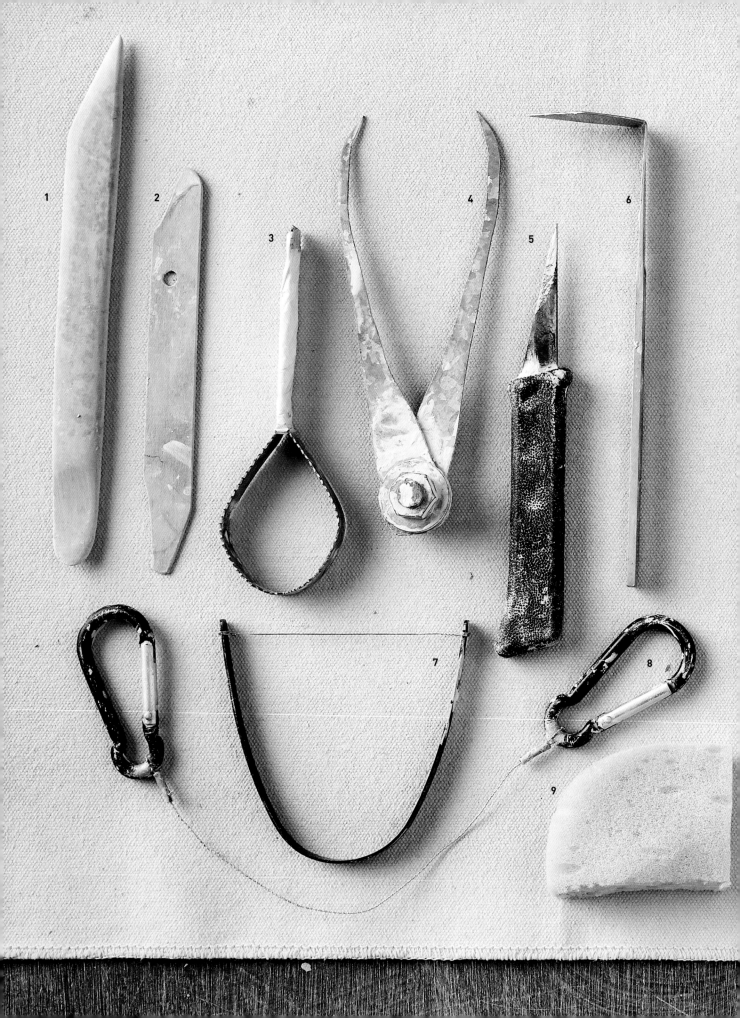

TOOLS

Having the right tool for the job is vital to getting a piece just how you want it and can save lots of time. I work with a combination of purchased and homemade tools. In fact, I'm a massive fan of making my own tools, as they're customized for exactly the job at hand. If making tools isn't something that interests you, then there are commercial alternatives to most of these. Although my toolbox is normally overflowing, these are the items I use most and couldn't work without.

1 POINTED WOODEN
MODELING TOOL
For refining surfaces, modeling decoration, and sealing joins. The curved end can be used to join seams. The pointy end can be used to trim the base of a pot in later throwing stages.

2 CARVED WIDE LOLLIPOP STICK
Shaped using an electric sander. The thinness of the stick makes it good for fettling (see Glossary, page 154) joins on handles, while the shapes are great for working in corners.

3 LOOPED SAW BLADE
A section of a bandsaw blade, shaped and bound with electrical tape. The serrated side can be used for scoring or refining lumpy surfaces. The flat side can be used as a looped turning tool (see Medium Looped Tool, page 49).

4 CALIPERS
I made these calipers, but there are better ones on the market, so I suggest you buy yours. Calipers are used as measuring guides, particularly for making lidded items.

5 POTTER'S KNIFE
This standard knife has a black molded plastic handle and a fine iron blade. The iron gets a bit rusty, giving the blade a fine saw tooth, which makes the knife a great cutting tool.

6 TRIMMING TOOL
I made this by cutting and grinding a knife "borrowed" from the canteen at the Royal College of Art, in London, and bending the end over. It is perfect for trimming and undercutting in the final stages of throwing.

7 BOW HARP
A one-handed wire allows you to cut against molds or profiles while holding the clay or rotating a banding wheel with the other hand.

8 CUTTING WIRE
I make my own with a length of twisted wire known as shell wire, which you can buy. Here, I've used two carabiners as handles, which are comfortable to use and easy to replace. I used a strip of plastic wire covering to cover the sharp ends of the twisted wire. I like a wire with a twist as it pulls air between the cut sides and aids release of the clay from its surface. These are available to buy, too.

9 THROWING SPONGE
Cut from a jumbo car sponge, it's possible to make eight throwing sponges from the two curved ends and a bigger sponge from the middle section. The shape is perfect because it has a curve for bowl interiors and a square edge for cylinders.

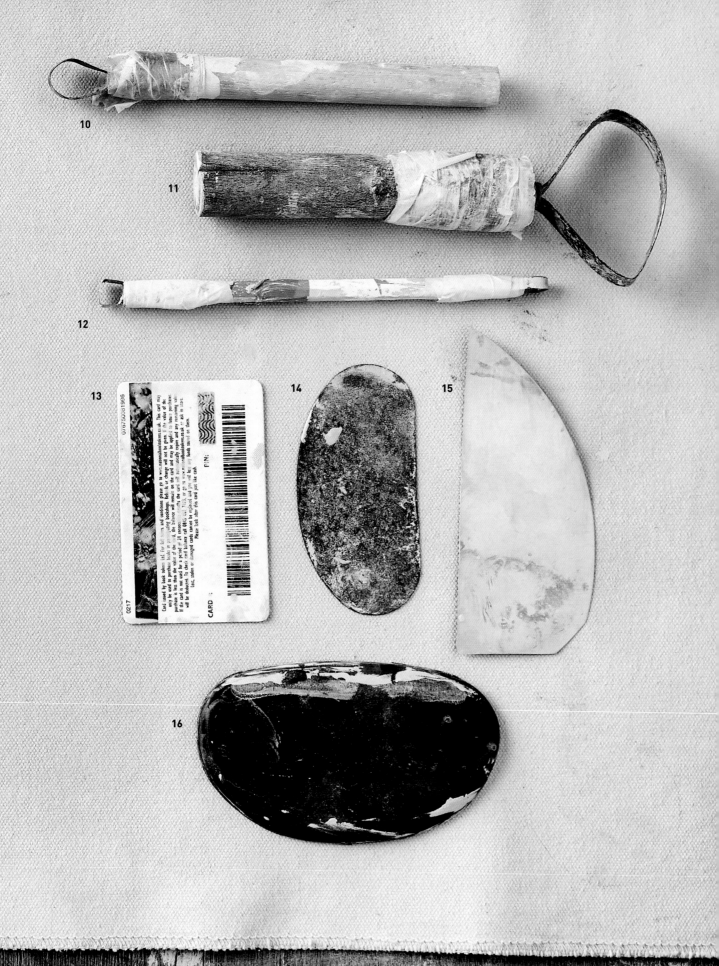

10 MEDIUM LOOPED TURNING TOOL

Used for trimming excess clay in the turning process. The loop allows the clay to flow through the tool as you trim away the excess. Made from metal package strapping and taped to a section of dowel, this is a hard-wearing, long-lasting, and easily replaceable tool. Finer steel versions are readily available in most tool sets.

11 LARGE, WIDE-LOOPED TURNING TOOL

As above, but fitted into a cut-in a section of a tree branch. It feels lovely in the hand. Again, similar tools are available for purchase. This tool is used for broad-surface turning.

12 SMALL AND SHARP LOOPED TURNING TOOL

Made from cut sections of a tin can, one bent into a square and the other into a round shape. These are then taped to either end of a pencil. The tin is razor-sharp and perfect for very accurate turning. The tin sections will need to be replaced fairly often and should be kept small, as they are too flexible when looped larger. Similar fine tools can be found, but they are not as common or as sharp.

13 CREDIT CARD

This very useful and easy-to-come-by tool can be used as a straight-sided rib or cut into shapes to make profiles for throwing.

14 METAL KIDNEY OR RIB (IRON)

The iron of this cutting and shaping tool gets a bit rusty, creating a fine saw tooth. This makes it great for cutting surfaces, but it can leave texture marks.

15 METAL KIDNEY OR RIB (STEEL)

A refining and burnishing tool used to finish surfaces. It should not be used as a cutting tool. Use the iron version for cutting instead.

16 RUBBER KIDNEY

Used mainly in hand building, the soft rubber palette blends the clay into a smooth and uniform surface.

USING A BAT

Anything can be thrown on a bat, but it is a necessity for plates and wide, shallow pieces. A bat is a wooden disk that is attached to the wheel head using the method described here. The idea is that you can throw a piece of any size or shape and leave it on the bat to dry. The bat with the pot attached is removed from the wheel head, freeing it up for the next pot.

The traditional way of attaching a bat is with a clay pad. The process of making this reusable pad is known as "batting out" and works universally with any potter's wheel. To begin, imagine you are going to make a plate about ½ inch (1 cm) thick, with the same diameter as your bat (roughly 2 pounds/1 kg of clay will do in most cases). Center a piece of medium to firm clay and open it out like a plate (see Plate, steps 1–2, page 85), so you have a flat pad of clay. Trim the edge of the pad so it is ½–¾ inch (1–2 cm) narrower than the diameter of the bat. This will allow you to get a tool underneath the clay to release the bat. Draw rings in the clay by spinning the wheel and holding your finger in place—three to four rings, roughly spread out, should suffice. The depth should be just over halfway through the clay pad. Finally, stop the wheel and draw a cross through the pad to the same depth (see image, right). This allows air into the rings and prevents total suction.

To attach the bat, rub over the back with a slightly damp sponge—not enough to make the bat wet, but just enough to change the clay's color. This will help it stick to the wheel head. Center the bat by tapping the sides of the bat while spinning the wheel. Once it is roughly in the middle, spin the wheel at a low to medium speed and hammer the center of the bat with the side of your fist multiple times (never bash either side or you'll squish the clay bat). It should now be attached and ready to use.

To remove the bat, slide a tool with an oblong edge underneath and twist. The bat should pop up, and you can then lift it off. A clay bat can be reused many times until it dries out.

WIRE AND LEAVE-ON BAT

For large or wide pieces, such as plates or serving dishes, or very thin pieces, wire the pots after throwing and leave them on the bat until they are firm enough to lift off. Follow the first wiring technique in the Cylinder section using a twisted wire, but do not lift (see step 14, page 68). For wide pieces, it can be a good idea to leave them slightly thicker in the middle as the wire will naturally rise up slightly over a wider surface as you're wiring. Be sure to keep the wire as taut as possible and wire through once only. If you're struggling to get the wire all the way through a very wide piece, try spinning the wheel very slowly and pulling your right hand firmly back toward you.

PLANNING A PROJECT

For all functional wares, there must be a design process. Whether you like planning the design or not, it is vitally important to the success of any object. For artistic production, it's easy to say there are no rules to follow, but that's a cop-out. The best artists do not simply create—they plan, sketch, and build maquettes, following a process as rigid as the functional designer.

During the design process, you decide and set the parameters for the piece, both physically and ideologically. These set parameters become the markers of success or failure in the final product. Design can be a physical process. It can involve testing, for example, at the wheel to see what weight of clay is needed, which belly suits what neck, what colors you can create in the glaze lab, and so on. However, the quickest and most effective design tools are pen and paper. Through quick sketches, you can try out multiple variations in seconds, and noting the jobs the piece needs to perform will help dictate its final function and form. Through refinement, these sketches and notes become the core of what the pot will be and the points to which quality (or success) can be attributed.

DESIGN CONSIDERATIONS:

- What is the piece for?
- How does it work?
- How does it feel?
- What are its volume and dimensions?
- Is it well-balanced?
- How does its foot meet the flat surface?
- Where does the inside end and outside start?
- Does the glaze/clay surface complement the form?
- What is the color palette? Is it an informed choice?
- Is the surface fit for the piece's purpose? Is it food-safe/scratch-resistant?
- Is it inviting?
- Is it a strong design?
- Is it quiet or loud?
- Where would it look best?
- Does it look cheap? Or expensive?
- How much can it be sold for?
- Which stores or galleries sell similar products?
- What products are similar on the market, and why are they successful?

CENTERING

Centering is the fundamental groundwork for all thrown ware. Think of it as the foundation of the piece. The process of centering is to make sure that the clay sits perfectly on the center of the wheel head. If the clay is a little off to one side, then, once a hole is pushed in the middle, one side will be thicker than the other, creating an unbalanced object.

1

If strong enough, you can wrestle the clay into the middle of the wheel. However, clay forced into the round like this is not really centered. Centered clay has been through a process of squeezing and pushing, using the action of the wheel, not only to make it round but also to align the particles within the clay into a spiral form—this is where thrown ware gets its strength. By using the process and your body correctly, anyone can center any reasonable weight of clay with a little practice.

The action of squeezing in, to bring the clay up, and pushing down, to reform the ball, forces the clay into the center and creates a unique alignment inside the clay at the same time. The process also compresses the clay, which is vital for preventing cracking during the drying process. The spiral form within allows the clay body to "untwist" a little in the intense heat of the kiln. This "flexibility" gives thrown ware durability for firing.

It is worth mastering centering before moving on to throwing a cylinder, bowl, or plate. Regard rushed or poor centering as a bad foundation, to be corrected before construction goes any further.

2

1 Before you place the clay on the wheel, clean and dry the wheel head or bat, if required. To do this, hold a damp sponge on its surface with the wheel spinning. Keep the wheel going and then use the side of your thumb as a squeegee to remove any scraps from the center out to the edge. The throwing surface should be dust-free, but never wet, before attaching the clay, as both dust and wetness can prevent the clay from adhering to the wheel head or bat.

2 With clean, dry hands, firmly pat the ball of clay onto the wheel head. You can maneuver the clay so it is approximately centered on the wheel head. With the wheel spinning slowly, quickly and repeatedly slap the clay from the top corner down toward the middle, supporting the bottom edge of the clay with your other hand. A roughly round, cone-like shape should begin to form. This is a good starting point.

3a

3b

3 Sponge a good amount of water over the ball and wet your hands. You need the wheel to be moving fast. Depending on the wheel you're using, you probably want it at full speed (3a). Place your hands in the "Hook and Anchor" position (see page 41). From the base of your right fingers, pull the clay back toward the left anchor. This squeezing motion brings the clay upward into a cone shape (3b). Do not try to lift the clay, as the inward squeeze will force it up. Be careful not to press your hands down against the wheel. This is a common way to steady yourself, but it will result in friction burn on the sides of your hands. Instead, allow them to touch the wheel without any downward pressure.

4 To bring the clay back down, raise your right hand so the center of the palm sits on the top right corner of the clay. Push over and down into the anchor, making sure the left hand is stable. Ensure your right hand is off-center, or it will get dragged around by the force of the wheel. Keep adding water if you feel the clay is drying out.

4

5

6

7

5 Repeat steps 3 and 4 as many times as it takes for the clay to feel centered—your fingers shouldn't feel like they're moving. Hold the clay steady for a few seconds as it rotates—it should feel very comfortable.

6 To check the clay is perfectly centered, hold your hand on top of it, as shown. You shouldn't see any movement in your fingers and will barely feel the clay moving. Here's a good rule to follow: if you're not sure, then it's not centered.

7 Use the "Karate Chop" hand position (see page 41) to compress and flatten the top of the clay to prepare to open it up.

CYLINDER

The cylinder is the basis of any upright form. The quality and capacity of cylinder production are often regarded as signs of a potter's skill. Once mastered, the steps almost become one fluid motion. Though many potters use measuring gauges to ensure their pieces are the same size, the hands of production potters can remember forms so well that they can re-create them to within millimeters of each other or even without thinking.

Mastering the cylinder will improve all aspects of your throwing. It is always where I encourage people to start and where I send them back if they're struggling. Being able to make a cylinder will open up a whole vocabulary of ceramics, as its variations are limitless. Look around you next time you're in a restaurant, café, or home store, and you'll likely find a ceramic cylinder. We live with the cylinder every day and, although it is often overlooked, it is a fundamental form for function and one any ceramicist must learn inside out. While there are many variations on the following techniques, this is the method I have developed over the past seventeen years. I have borrowed and adapted methods from some of the greatest studio potters in the UK and apply them to my work on a daily basis. Find your own way through, if you wish, but trust in these guidelines and you won't go wrong.

1 GOING IN

▷ **Using "Pint Glass" and "Cub Scouts" hand positions (see pages 41 and 42)**

Once you've centered your clay, use your left thumb as a bridge to support your right hand and place two fingers in the center of the clay. In other words, send the scouts over the bridge to find the middle. Gently apply pressure until you feel a small point running between your index and middle fingers. Take time to check you're in the center of the clay, as a hole that's not in the middle is as bad as an uncentered pot. Apply pressure from the pads of the fingertips, not the ends. The ends of your fingers should bend back slightly against the pressure on the clay. This compresses the clay rather than cuts it. It takes quite a lot of force and will feel strange the first time you do it properly. You need to be sure the clay is squeezed down into the base, as this makes it much stronger and will stop it from cracking later (see S-cracks in Faults and Flaws, page 151). Try to make the base ½–⅝ inch (1–1.5 cm) thick, depending how the vessel will be finished. This will become second nature over time, but you can check the thickness by pushing a pin through the base. Slide your finger down the pin until it touches the clay and then pull it out, keeping your finger beside it. The length of the pin below your finger is the thickness of the base.

1

2 OPENING OUT

Once the center has been pushed down to the correct depth, swing the "Pint Glass" left hand around, so it is directly in front of you at the 6 o'clock position. Straighten up the "Cub Scouts" right hand on the inside and, as one unit, pull back toward yourself. Be careful not to squeeze the left and right hands together at this point. Open out the base ¾–1¼ inches (2–3 cm) wider than it needs to be.

3 CLEANING AND COMPRESSING THE BASE

Hold a sponge between the inside of the fingers and your right thumb. Press the sponge into the base and allow the end of the sponge to sit under your fingertips to increase the surface area of the fingers' pressure. Firmly work back and forth from the center of the base to the 5 o'clock position to flatten, tidy, and compress the base. Be careful not to apply too much pressure, as you could thin the base.

2

3

4

4 BRINGING IT IN
▷ **Using "Thumbs Up" hand position (see page 42)**

Hold your hands on either side of the pot and gently squeeze inward until the inside of the cylinder is the required width. This gives the base of the wall strength and creates a good internal angle between the base and the wall. Always concentrate on the internal width at this stage, not the external dimensions, as the thickness of the wall, which will be lifted to give the wall height, misrepresents the width of the cylinder.

5 LIFTING UP
▷ **Using "Crab Claw and Trigger Finger" hand position (see page 43)**

Gently squeeze from your outside index finger toward the inside one (5a). Apply firm pressure at the bottom of the inside wall where you are also pushing against the base of the pot. Start from the very bottom of the wall and squeeze gently as you draw your hands slowly up the wall (5b). It'll be easier to lift the clay as you move up the wall; make sure your movements are measured so the thickness of the wall will be even. You'll need to do this two or three times to move the majority of the clay up before changing hand positions. The wall at the bottom of the pot will be slightly thicker than at the top to provide support.

NOTE Keep the wall wet at all times and use a medium to fast wheel speed with slow-moving hands. Thrown rings should look more like grooves on a record than spirals.

5a

5b

6 COLLARING

▷ **Using "Triangle Hands" hand position (see page 44)**

Collaring is the process of bringing the width of the pot in to the desired proportions. Here, you are using it to keep the cylinder narrow. This is a preventative measure, as it's easy for the clay to flare out while lifting. The process can be repeated throughout the lifting stages (steps 5 and 7–10), to keep the form contained. Form a triangle with your thumbs and index fingers. Start from the bottom of the pot with flat hands, adding a finger at a time to the triangle as you draw your hands up toward the rim. It is best to do this at a medium to fast wheel speed and with slow hands. If the rim ripples up, you're doing too much at once; if it becomes uneven, you can trim it with a pin (see step 11, page 66).

7 WEIGHT LIFTING

▷ **Using "Tip to Tip" hand position (see page 43)**

One of the most common problems with thrown ware is a heavy bottom. We've already started to prevent this by concentrating on the internal width when we made the base. Now, in the lifting stage, you will utilize all the excess clay at the base of the wall to create lots of extra height. With the wheel at medium speed, create an undercut in the base with the right middle finger by holding it horizontally and with the nail facing the spinning wheel.

6

7

8

9

8 Place the fingers of your left hand against the inside of the pot. Mirror this with the right hand on the outside. Try to touch your thumbs together where possible to stabilize the hands and make them move as one unit. Do not try to "lift" the clay, as it will pull off; instead, with the pad of the right middle finger, squeeze firmly inward against the middle finger on the left hand.

9 Gradually move your hands up the wall, attempting to keep your hands and arms as steady as possible. Allow the inside hand to lead by just a fraction ahead of the outside hand. Bear in mind that as you move up the wall away from the base, you will need less pressure because the clay is thinner.

NOTE You must complete each lift through to the rim to ensure the sides of the vessel are uniform.

10 USING A RIB

▷ **Using "Tip to Rib" hand position
(see page 43)**

In this step, you will compress, straighten,
clean off, and tidy up the wall. When throwing,
I suggest using a wooden rib to lift the clay
(normally this can be done with fingers).
Otherwise, I always use an iron rib. Hold the
rib perpendicular to the wheel head, but
angle it so that the clay slips off it slightly.
Place the left hand on the inside of the pot.
While the right hand holds the rib firmly at
the base of the pot, slide the left hand slowly
up the inside. Move the rib only when the pot
is bigger than the rib. (As a beginner, it is
more common to throw a shorter cylinder,
such as a mug.) For this example, once the
inside hand has reached the top of the rib,
slowly begin to move the rib in unison with
the inside hand. When you begin lifting the
rib above the base, angle the bottom of the
rib slightly closer to you and the top farther
away. Be sure to lift your inside hand and rib
all the way to the rim.

LEFT Throwing a cylinder at
the wheel using the tip to tip
hand position.

11 TRIMMING A RIM

With the wheel moving at low to medium speed, hold the rim lightly between the index finger and thumb of your left hand. Place a pin or the tip of a sharp knife on the tip of your thumb. Hold the tool firmly, as it can snag on the pot while the wheel rotates. You will need to remove a minimum of ³⁄₁₆ inch (5 mm) from the top of the rim, or the rim will buckle— about ½ inch (1 cm) is ideal. Slowly push the tool into the clay, just enough to score it at first, and then a little more until you feel it touch against your left index finger (11a). Allow the wheel to rotate once fully and then lift. Hopefully, the trimming will come away in one piece but, if it doesn't, you may have to remove it carefully by hand (11b).

11a

11b

12

13

12 SPONGING
▷ **Using "Edge Fingers" hand position (see page 44)**

This step can be useful at many stages during the throwing process to compress the rim and give it a bit more strength before stretching. Here, however, you will be using it in the "final throws." Hold the rim gently between the index finger and thumb of your left hand, then place a sponge on the tip edge. Hold the sponge in the right hand and guide it with the right index or middle finger while the wheel spins. This will help to straighten and smooth the rim, clean off excess slurry, and compress the clay. Don't overdo it! Many a pot has been lost by fiddling with the rim. A lot can be rectified by a little sponging at the leather-hard stage (see page 92), so don't risk the pot to correct that little dot on the rim.

13 UNDERCUTTING

Before wiring a pot, it is good practice to undercut the base slightly with a pointy tool. There are hundreds of variations of pointy tools. Here, I'm using one I made myself from a sharpened canteen knife bent with a vice. The idea is to gently remove the last bit of weight from the base. It also leaves a slight shadow gap under the foot of the pot, which makes it look light and almost as if it is floating on a surface. Another benefit is that it creates a defined line, which you can use to clean the glaze off later. It also reduces the chance of glazes sticking to the kiln shelf because they have slightly farther to run. Finally, it simply makes it easier to get the wire underneath, so it's worth doing even if you're going to trim the base (see Turning, pages 92–103).

14a

14b

14 WIRING AND LIFTING

For items that can be lifted from the wheel straight after throwing, this can be a time-saving technique. It is ideal for narrow items such as cylinders or small bowls. Clean any slurry from the outside of the pot with a metal kidney, then clean and dry your hands.

Ideally, you should use a twisted wire, known as shell wire. This will add a texture to the base of the pot and allow in a little air, which helps the pot separate from the wheel. If you dry-cut with a smooth wire, you may find the clay sticks back together after the wire passes through. Hold the wire firmly in both hands and stretch to create tension. Push your thumbs into the wire to stretch it. Place your thumbs on the wheel head (or bat) behind the pot and pull back through the base toward you (14a). Carefully grasp the base of the pot and lift it away from the wheel head (14b). Gently place the pot on a board to dry. You can put many pots on the same board with this technique, saving lots of valuable shelf space for drying.

15a

15b

15 WIRING AND SLIDING

This technique is ideal for more awkwardly shaped pieces, such as wider bowls, bellied forms, or thin pots. Squeeze some water around the pot and, with a smooth wire held in the same way as for step 14, pull the wire under the pot two or three times (15a). You should feel the pot move a little on the second or third pull. The wiring pulls water under the pot and creates a slippery film.

Take a small work board and wet the area you wish to slide the pot onto. This will prevent the pot from sticking before it's fully on the board. Place your hand flat on the wheel head (or bat) with the palm facing upward. Cup the base of the pot with the side of your palm and little finger. Twist the pot as you pull it toward the board. Hold the board a millimeter or so below the edge of the wheel head and carefully slip the pot onto the board (15b).

Try to use a board with an absorbent surface, so the pot can dry from underneath. Handle the board with care because the pot may still be slippery.

Variations

STRAIGHT SIDED – MUG / BEAKER / UTENSIL HOLDER

This variation simply changes the height of the basic cylinder. You control the height by changing the weight of the clay used. Always work from the internal diameter to avoid leaving excess clay in the base. The outside of the cylinder can be trimmed during throwing or later in the turning process. In the later stages, use a wooden or metal rib instead of your hands to throw. This will straighten the wall. For a mug, you can add a handle at the leather-hard stage (see page 107).

SHALLOW AND WIDE – SQUARED BOWL / SERVING DISH

In addition to having all the elements of the straight-sided cylinder, this low, squared dish is much wider at the base, creating a form that is broader than it is tall. Be careful to leave the base thick enough to ensure you can compress it adequately. If you require a square dish with a base wider than an average side plate, it may be more practical to follow the steps for making a plate (see pages 84–89), but rather than making a plate rim, simply pull the wall like you would when making a cylinder. Following the plate technique would provide better compression over a broader surface area. You can refine the outside and underside when turning.

SHOULDER AND LIP – VASE / JAR / PITCHER

To add a shoulder to a cylinder, place your hands in the "Tip to Tip" hand position (see page 43), use the inside hand to gently push outward and the outside hand to control how quickly the clay flares. Do not squeeze the clay or let the wall get too thin before pushing out. You can refine the shoulder using a metal rib, flexed to match the outside curve of the shoulder. Once the shoulder is the desired width, remove your inner hand and use the collaring technique (see step 6, page 62) to bring in the neck of the piece. Then, using a metal rib, gently refine the shape working on the outside only, to ensure flowing forms with no sagging areas. Once you've refined the form, you can turn over the top to create a lip. With the wheel at medium to slow speed, place a vertical index finger on the inside of the neck and move the finger to a horizontal position to gently turn out the rim.

ENCLOSED FORM – BOTTLE / BUD VASE / MOON JAR / TEAPOT

To make an enclosed form, you must throw a narrow cylinder and make the area to be "bellied" out thicker. This thickness will be spread out as the pot stretches. If the walls of the cylinder are too thin, it will collapse as you push outward. To "belly" out, use the "Tip to Tip" hand position (see page 43). Do not squeeze the clay. Simply use the inside hand to push outward gently and the outside hand to control how quickly the clay flares. You can refine this area using a metal rib that is flexed to match the curve on the outside. It is better to refine gradually, repeating the process multiple times, than do too much too quickly. Once the belly is the desired width, you can remove the inner hand and use the collaring technique (see step 6, page 62) to bring in the neck of the piece. The clay may ripple and need trimming. Again, it is better to do this gradually than try to do it all at once.

WIDE BASE TAPERED – PITCHER / POURER / STEM VASE

For a wide base that tapers to a narrow neck, open up the base to increase the internal width. The external width is deceptive, as it contains the thickness of the clay to be lifted. When lifting up, angle your hands inward. Once you've lifted the weight up into the wall, use the collaring technique (see step 6, page 62) to bring the neck in to the width you want. Use a metal rib to refine the shape from the outside only, to ensure a flowing form with no sagging areas. To make a pouring lip, take the pot off the wheel. While it is still wet, dampen an index finger and place the pad at the edge of the rim, just inside it. Turn your finger from a vertical position to a horizontal one, and twist lightly from side to side to increase the width of the lip, if required. If your finger is too dry, it will stick to and tear the rim. If the rim is too thin or overstretched, it will also probably tear. Use a thumb or wide tool for a larger lip.

BOWL

---

*A bowl is perhaps the most common form in functional
ceramics. It comes in all shapes and sizes, from a cup to
a sink, but the theory behind its form remains the same:
it is practical and ergonomic, an open vessel,
and a functional container.*

Some of my favorite pots are housed in the British Museum's Korean Collection. Though they are 2,000 years old, they use exactly the same principles and tools as we do today. Technology has moved on light years since then, but only the addition of a motor to a wheel has changed the technique. Those finely thrown bowls have seen generations come and go, yet still have the same strength and resonance today as they did when they first came out of the kiln.

It's worth having a good think about what it is you want to make before you get started, as the design of your form will alter your starting position. I like to throw thin, delicate tableware, and the following method is an example of how to get the most from your clay. If you want to make something with a little more robustness, strength, or weight, I suggest you try to make a thin bowl first so you see where it needs strength and weight for balance. Then increase the weight of clay you use without increasing the scale of the bowl. This way, you will truly understand the form and make considered choices.

TIP If you intend to make a wide, shallow bowl, you may want to look at the techniques in the Plate section (see pages 84–89) and consider alternating between the instructions where relevant.

1

1 GOING IN
▷ **Using "Pint Glass" and "Cub Scouts" hand positions (see page 41 and 42)**

This first stage is the same as that used for a cylinder (see Cylinder, steps 1–3, pages 59–60), but use three fingers to create the hole. Using your left thumb as a bridge to support the right hand, run three fingers in toward the center of the clay. Remember: send the scouts over the bridge to find the middle. Gently apply pressure until you feel a small point running between your index and middle fingers. Take time to be certain you're in the center of the clay.

Apply pressure from the pads of your fingertips, not the ends. The ends of the fingers will bend back slightly as you press the clay. This creates compression. It takes quite a lot of force and will feel strange the first time you do it properly. You need to be sure the clay is squeezed down into the base, as this makes it much stronger and will stop it from cracking later (see S-cracks in Faults and Flaws, page 151). Try to make the base ½–⅝ inch (1–1.5 cm) thick, depending on whether it will be turned or not. The thicker the base, the better for turning, particularly if you intend to make a foot ring.

2a

2b

3

2 OPENING OUT

Once the center has been pushed down to the correct depth, swing the "Pint Glass" left hand around so it is directly in front of you at the 6 o'clock position (2a). Keep the pads of the inside fingers flat against the clay and start to pull both hands, as one, back toward you. Your fingers will bend back slightly at the tip, forming a perfect curve as the bowl reaches the desired width. Gently pull the inside fingers up the wall to continue the curve of the inside wall (2b). Be careful not to squeeze the left and right hands together at this point.

3 CLEANING AND COMPRESSING THE BASE

Hold a sponge with your right thumb against the inside of your fingers. Press the sponge into the base and allow the end of the sponge to sit under your fingertips to increase the surface area of the fingers' pressure. Work back and forth over the curved interior near the base, applying enough pressure to compress the clay but not so much as to thin the base.

4

4 LIFTING UP

▷ **Using "Crab Claw and Trigger Finger" hand positions (see page 43)**

This first stage of lifting is very similar to that used for a cylinder (see Cylinder, step 5, page 61), as you want to lift the weight out of the base straight up the wall. Try to keep the form contained, but don't worry if it flares out a little as it will be opened up eventually anyway. With a medium wheel speed and the outside index finger, gently squeeze toward the inside index finger. Apply firm pressure at the bottom where you are also pushing against the base of the pot. This is particularly tough in a bowl

because the interior is curved, which leaves more weight in the bottom. Try not to spoil the curve on the inside and make sure most of the applied pressure comes from the outside.

Start from the very bottom of the wall and squeeze gently as you draw your hands slowly upward. It will be easier to lift the clay as you move up the wall; make sure to use measured movements so the thickness of the wall will be even. Repeat this two or three times before changing hand positions.

5 WEIGHT LIFTING
▷ **Using "Tip to Tip" hand position (see page 43)**
This step will help you get the most from your clay and avoid as much trimming as possible later on. If you do not intend to trim the pot, it is vital to get as much weight out of the base at this stage as possible. Start by undercutting the base by holding your right middle finger with the nail against the spinning wheel.

6 Place your left fingers against the inside of the pot. Mirror this with your right hand on the outside. Try to touch your thumbs together where possible to stabilize the hands and make them move as one unit. Do not try to "lift" the clay, as it will pull off. Instead, with the pad of your right middle finger, squeeze firmly inward against the middle finger on the left hand.

7 Gradually move your hands up the wall, attempting to keep your hands and arms as steady as possible. Allow the inside hand to lead just a fraction ahead of the outside hand. Bear in mind that as you move up the wall away from the base, you will need less pressure because the clay is thinner. Again, try to maintain the internal curve in the base. You can allow the clay to flare out slightly with each lift.

NOTE Leave enough thickness in the wall at this stage to continue the thinning process in step 8.

5

6

8
—

9
—

8 OPENING OUT THE BOWL
▷ **Using "Tip to Rib" hand position
(see page 44)**

Before opening the bowl out, it's a good idea
to compress the rim a little. To do this, hold
the rim between the index finger and thumb of
your left hand and, using a sponge or a finger
on the right hand, push the rim down and in.

To open the bowl in three movements. I like
to use a square iron kidney and hold it in my
right hand, but you can form a straight "rib"
by aligning the fingertips. Either way, you
want to cover a fairly broad surface area on
the outside to support the wall and prevent
it from buckling.

Place the rib vertically on the outside of the
pot, with the right hand at the 3 o'clock
position on the wheel face and the fingers of
the left hand on the inside. Push the wall out
by one-third of the way to its final width.
Repeat this step twice.

9 With the inside hand, push it against the
outside hand. Draw the two hands up the
sides of the bowl. Do not panic at the rim.
It may seem as if it is turning in over your
fingers, but just keep going and the clay will
follow. You are only shaping the bowls, so
there should be no squeezing.

TIP Watch that the rim isn't getting too thin—a
little compression between pushes can
prevent splitting.

10

10 FINISHING THE INSIDE

▷ **Using "Back-handed Kidney" hand position (see page 45)**

Once you have the outside form as you want it, hold the curved edge of a kidney on the inside wall to create a seamless curve (where desired) between the base and wall. Placing the right hand in the left side of the bowl gives you more dexterity in the wrist. The clay will pull off the rib backward, but this gives you greater control of the curve. You may want to set up a mirror behind the wheel so you can see the curve in profile. This will save your back by preventing you from leaning over. If your rims turn in during drying, this is a good opportunity to push them out slightly to combat this common problem.

NOTE See Cylinder, steps 11–15, pages 66–69, for guidance on trimming, sponging, undercutting, wiring, lifting, and sliding.

Variations

LIPPED BOWL – SERVING / SOUP / CEREAL / SALAD / DESSERT

A lip can be an aesthetic and practical addition to a form. The throwing process for this variation is the same as the one for a bowl. Leave enough weight in the rim so that you have enough clay to turn out the lip. To turn out the lip, place a vertical index finger on the inside of the rim with the wheel at medium to slow speed and gently turn the rim over by moving your finger into a horizontal position. You may find it useful to support the clay on the outside, just under the rim, as it begins to flare. This can be done with a finger or thumb in a comfortable, well-steadied position.

WIDE SHALLOW DISH – PASTA / SALAD / SOUP

If a wider surface is required, it is worth thinking about the curve where the internal space meets the inside base. It is difficult to get a continuous curve over a broad area without thinning the base too much. A flat bottom is a more practical shape for production. For very wide shallow dishes, you may want to use the techniques used for a plate. This form is quite often not turned and can be trimmed in the end stages of throwing.

DEEP BROAD FOOTED BOWL
– MIXING / SALAD

When you require a stable bowl for mixing ingredients or large salads, a deeper form with a wider foot is best. The foot helps prevent movement, and the depth reduces spillage during mixing. I would suggest making the wall of a mixing bowl extra thick if you're going to use it to beat with a whisk or crack eggs on the rim. The extra weight will also improve stability.

SMALL DEEP BOWL – TEA BOWL / COFFEE CUP

A small bowl can be the ideal vessel for hot drinks. It is more comfortable to hold than a straight cylinder. The tea bowl shows a traditional interaction between human and ceramics, steeped in history and ceremony. With the addition of a handle, it can become a cup. Wider and thinner bowls will cool a hot drink more quickly. If you are not adding a handle, it is advisable to allow the drink to cool first or fill the bowl only two-thirds of the way up, so you can hold it by the rim.

TALL AND NARROW BOWL – VASE / CENTERPIECE / STORAGE JAR

This piece draws on the skills used for both a cylinder and bowl. While the form has a curved interior and exterior like a bowl, its elongated proportions mean the clay must be lifted up and contained more during throwing. It is not "opened out" as much as other bowls, so it is ideal to make the rim thinner during throwing, as when making a cylinder.

PLATE

---

*Plates are perhaps the most functional and durable
of all tableware. We put them through a lot on a daily basis.
They have to be tough enough to withstand instant heat from
food or warming, pressure from cutlery, stacking,
and frequent washing.*

Often overlooked, the plate is the basis of all tableware collections, but making them by hand can prove difficult. As a result, plates are often mass-produced and accented by other handmade items. Having produced hundreds, if not thousands, of thrown plates, I believe they are special and a joy to create. I love the process of making plates. I recommend soft clay (unless you want a wide, flat rim). Because soft clay is more malleable, it requires less working than firmer clay. The basic processes of throwing a plate are similar to those of throwing a cylinder and bowl. However, I'm going to demonstrate quite a different way of opening up a plate that will take some getting used to, but it shows how the body is an ideal tool for throwing.

1 GOING IN / OPENING OUT
▷ **Using the "Fist Press" hand position (see page 45)**

Center the clay. Adopt the "Fist Press" hand position, putting the side of your right fist against the middle of the clay. Use an open left hand to support the outside of the clay and begin to push down with your fist. The clay will start to spread. Hold your wrist and the base of your right arm in place and push with the fist as the clay spreads.

2 Once the fist is the desired depth (about ⅝–¾ inch /1.5–2 cm from the wheel head), start to pull it back toward you. The bone in the side of your hand acts like a straight wooden rib and the squashed heel like a flexible rubber kidney. As you get closer to the edge, a lump will form at the wrist, just behind the fist; this leaves enough clay to pull a rim. Repeat more than once by gently lifting the fist away and moving it back to the center to even out the surface and compress the clay. At the desired diameter, hold the position for a few seconds while the wheel spins at a medium to fast speed to even out the form, and lift your hand.

3 LIFTING THE RIM

▷ **Using the "Tip to Tip" hand position (see page 43)**

As with the "weight-lifting" sections for a cylinder and bowl, start by undercutting the base with your right middle finger, holding it horizontally against the base and with the nail facing the wheel. Push in a little to create a "wall." This will become the rim. Place your left fingers inside the rim, leading with the middle finger and supporting it with the others. Mirror this with your right hand on the outside of the rim. Touch the thumbs together to stabilize your hands and make them move as one unit. With the pad of your right middle finger, squeeze firmly inward against its mirror on the left. Gradually move your fingers up, keeping your hands and arms as steady as possible. Bear in mind that as you move up from the base, you will need less pressure because the clay is thinner. Take the "wall" as high as you want the rim to be wide.

TIP While the rim is vertical you have good access to the base, so this is an ideal time to tidy up and undercut it for wiring (see Cylinder, steps 13–15, pages 67–69).

4 OPENING OUT THE RIM

▷ **Using the "Back-handed Kidney" hand position (see page 45)**

Working on the inside of the rim on the left side, use the rib with the tip facing slightly toward you, so the clay is sliding along it. Use the curve of the kidney to open out the rim and blend it into the plate's surface. If you want to make a flat rim, use the flat side of the kidney to turn the rim out.

3

4

5

5 CLEANING, FINISHING, AND COMPRESSING THE SURFACE

Keeping the metal kidney in the same position, use the flat side to smooth and compress the base from the middle out to the 9 o'clock position. Use the curves of the tool to merge the base to the rim seamlessly, or to shape a stepped rim. Often with a plate, the rim may need a trim because the clay has been spread over a large surface area. Carefully wire through the base and leave the plate to dry to a firm leather-hard state before lifting from the bat.

NOTE See Cylinder, steps 11–15, pages 66–69 for guidance on trimming, sponging, undercutting, wiring, lifting, and sliding.

BELOW A curved rim plate. The surface is seamlessly blended into the rim. This form can be used for all sizes.

Variations

WIDE FLAT RIM PLATE

A stepped flat rim can be achieved by lifting the "wall" upright and leaving enough clay in the rim to stretch as it opens out. To turn out a lip by hand, with the wheel at medium to slow speed, place a vertical index finger on the inside of the rim and move the finger to a horizontal position. You many find it useful to support the clay on the outside just under the rim as it begins to flare. To turn out the rim with a rib, simply place the straight edge of a curved metal kidney against the inside of the lifted "wall" and slowly move the rib from a vertical to horizontal position. The depth of the step to the rim or the angle the rim takes is dictated by how far you go with this process. Firmer clay will help stop the rim from flopping during turning out. A rim such as this is good for containing liquids and provides an accessible, clear area to carry the plate.

COUPE-BOWL / PLATE

A coupe bowl or plate has a continuous curve from the rim to the middle. It is a difficult form to throw and requires more clay and turning. Extra clay is needed during throwing to account for the deep base and it can be a very deceptive form visually. You will need to utilize skills from the bowl and plate throwing processes to master a coupe, keeping the curve of a bowl while working on a broad surface area like a plate. I would suggest keeping the base thick and using the turning process to take out the excess weight later.

FLAT RIMLESS PLATE / SERVING DISH / CUTTING BOARD

Sometimes used for aesthetic purposes, a plate without a rim can bring an interesting visual element to food serving and is often used by food photographers because it doesn't "interfere with the subject." A rimless plate can also be used as a chopping board or cheese plate, and makes a nice surface for easy-access cutting, with no rim to catch your fingers. Simply pull the clay all the way out to the desired width and trim to size.

VERTICAL OR FLARED STRAIGHT-EDGED PLATE

This piece has the base of a plate, but the wall of a cylinder, giving it more volume and making it a better container for wet foods. Combine the opening of a plate with the lifting and finishing of a cylinder.

FLUTED RIM PLATE

How you want the rim to meet the plate is up to you. This process can be used with any of the variations shown here. Once the plate is made, use a wet finger to pick points to lift the rim back up. The number of flutes will be dictated by how much you can push the clay before it splits. It can be a good idea to let the rim dry off a little before trying this—but if it is too dry, the rim will crack when manipulated. I suggest making one flute and then adding another opposite to it—so 12 o'clock and 6 o'clock—then filling in with flutes at 9 and 3 o'clock (or north, south, east, and west). Fill the remaining gaps by placing the flutes in the center of these spaces. This will ensure even spacing.

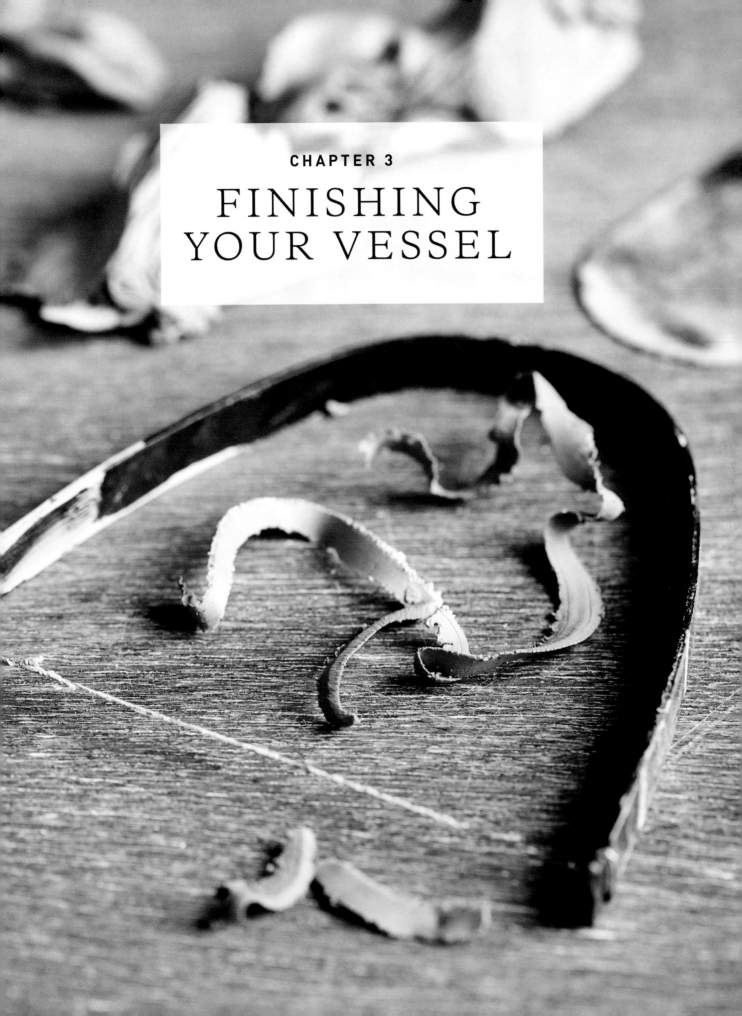

CHAPTER 3
FINISHING YOUR VESSEL

TURNING

Turning, also known as trimming, is the process of refining a pot at the leather-hard stage. The clay should be dry enough to support the shape of the pot throughout the turning process, but damp enough to work on and easily carve. We call this "leather-hard" in reference to the clay's feel and look: you should be able to handle it easily, without distorting the shape, but it should still look darker in color and feel cold to the touch.

Turning and refining is the process of removing clay to create practical and aesthetic features, such as a foot ring, or decorative details. It's a good idea to consider what kind of base you want the pot to have before the throwing stage, as this will inform how and where you may leave weight. For wider, deep bowls, for example, it might make sense to leave a bit of excess weight around the base to provide support for the walls during throwing. Knowing that this will be trimmed off later can speed up the throwing process and make it easier to concentrate on the internal form.

Turning is not essential to all forms. If you wish to make something that is simply flat-bottomed, you can skip this stage. However, I recommend a little hand finishing using ribs and a sponge to the underside of anything that isn't going to be refined on the wheel.

In my own work, I have found turning to be vital for refining delicate forms. I try to be as economical in my throwing as possible to leave less clay to remove during turning. When beginning any new form, I suggest you try one with and one without a turned foot, and see what marries and complements the form best for the most pleasing results.

TURNING TO CREATE A FOOT RING

Here I demonstrate the principles of creating a foot ring using a bowl. A foot ring is the circle of clay at the base of a pot that raises the form from the surface it's standing on. This technique is transferable to all forms—you simply apply the process to a broader surface.

BELOW A turned bowl with foot ring.

Place your leather-hard bowl back onto the wheel upside down and recenter it. There are two common methods of centering: marked and tap centering. I suggest, where possible, that you place the pot directly on the wheel head rather than use a bat. This ensures a true and level working surface. Most wheel heads have rings engraved in them. This is a great guide for starting, as you can use the rings to align your pot roughly in the center. Make sure the wheel head is clean, dry, and dust-free, then place the pot on its rim aligned as centrally as possible.

MARKED CENTERING

1 Set the wheel spinning at a slow speed. The pot is not attached to the wheel head, so it's imperative that you don't move the wheel too quickly or it will fly off. Hold a sharp knife or pin in your hand, grasping it close to the tip. Be sure to steady your body by tucking in your elbows and perhaps resting your forearms on the wheel tray or your thighs. Use your spare hand to support and steady the one gripping the tool. Carefully bring the point of the tool to the side of the pot without touching it, then allow the wheel to rotate a few times as you bring the point closer. This is a very slow movement of the hand. Eventually, the point will catch on the pot where it is off-center and leave a line on the surface—this should be a gentle score and not a cut into the pot.

2 Bring the wheel to a stop and turn the wheel head (not the pot) so the scored mark is sitting directly in front of you. Place your thumbs near the rim of the pot and gently push the pot back just a millimeter or two. This should move the pot closer to the center. Repeat steps 1 and 2 until you feel the scored mark is even all the way around the pot. Move the point of your tool up or down each time, so you can see each new line. If your pot is not perfectly round, or has been handled when damp, you may not get a perfect ring of a line. In this case, use your judgment to get the pot as close to centered as possible.

1

2

TAP CENTERING

This process works by utilizing the centripetal force of the spinning wheel. Each time you tap, you unbalance the pot and the force pulls it into the middle. Be careful not to get carried away with the speed of the wheel or the force of your tap, as the pot is liable to shoot off. I suggest practicing with something that's not precious until you get the feel for this.

1 Steady your body, as for Marked Centering (see page 95). Hover your left hand over the top left corner of the pot, set the wheel spinning at a medium to slow speed, and allow the fingertips of your left hand to feel the pot moving. With your right hand, use the tips of the index and middle fingers together, around a third of the way up the pot from the wheel head, then tap the pot just firmly enough for it to move a fraction. You should tap about every two seconds and, with practice, you will naturally feel when to do so. The pot will be centered when it is running smoothly against the tips of the left fingers and not "skipping."

If you're still unsure when to tap, a good analogy that I learned was to think of it like a musical beat. Every time the pot catches the fingers of your left hand is a beat, and you need to tap on the offbeat. So, a little like this: remember, the left hand is a beat and the right hand is a tap. Start by feeling the rhythm, (beat – beat – beat – beat – beat...), then add the tap between the beats, (beat – tap – beat – tap – beat – tap).

1

ATTACHING THE POT

2 Hold the pot in place by applying pressure on the base. You need to hold the pot firmly without damaging the rim. Roll a sausage of clay and push it down onto the wheel head at the rim of the pot. Try not to push the clay into the pot, as it will distort the rim or even displace the pot from the center. The idea is to attach the clay to the wheel and in turn secure the pot in place. For wider pieces, three evenly spaced sausages of clay will suffice; for smaller pieces, you can add clay all the way around.

SMOOTHING THE BASE

3 When wiring a pot or moving it onto a board, it's easy for the base to be a bit uneven. If you go straight at it with a broad tool, you'll find that the lumps and bumps make it difficult to cut a flat surface. To tackle this, you will use the corner tip of a small looped tool. This means you're working on a very small surface area at any time, which makes your movements more effective and stronger. Hold the tool like a pen and think of the right-hand corner as the nib. That is your point of contact. Steady your body and hands as you did for marked centering (see page 95). Place your left hand in the same position as for tap centering, stick out your thumb to meet the tool, and make contact between your two hands—this will make you much steadier.

Begin in the center of the base, and angle the tool so the cut clay can loop through the hole. With the wheel at high speed, carve in 1–2 mm. Keep your hands very steady and begin to pull the tool out to the 4 o'clock position. The rings you cut into the surface should be more like those on a record than a visible spiral. Once you have carved over the whole base, you should see that, although it is textured from the tool marks, it is now flat when viewed from the side. You may need to repeat this once or twice for very uneven bottoms.

2

3

CARVING THE FOOT RING

4 Switch to the broader edge of the turning tool, or consider using a broader tool to remove the tool marks (as for starting a flat base, see page 102). This will give you a good surface to work on. Now use the corner of a small looped turning tool, just as in step 3. Decide where you want your foot to be. Remember how the pot will be seen on the table: if the foot is too narrow, not only will the pot be unstable, but the foot can also disappear from sight under the wall. This is a shame if it's important to the form. A general rule of thumb is that the foot should be one third of the diameter of the rim. Once you've decided, mark the position of the foot by cutting grooves on either side of its chosen position. This is done so that its parameters are clearly set. When performing a moving cutting action, it is difficult to stop or start in a perfect circle, but these markers will guide you.

5 Using the same small tool and starting from the outside of the foot ring, cut the clay down so the foot stands at the height you want. Moving outward, cut the excess clay away as you blend the foot ring into the wall. This is a very satisfying moment, as lots of clay trimmings loop off the pot—exercise some caution so you don't get carried away.

4

5

CARVING OUT THE FOOT

6 Return to the middle of the pot and repeat step 3, only this time remove more clay as you move the tool out to meet the inside edge of the foot ring. (Having a good feel of the pot before you begin turning will give you a sense of how much clay to remove.) You may wish to do this two or three times, removing a little at a time rather than trying to take it all off at once. This is often the thinnest part of the pot.

7 Use the broad parts of the turning tool and switch to a broader tool where possible to remove some of the cutting marks and the marks from the marked centering, if you used this technique. Always try to work outward, whether from the center of the foot or from the foot to the side. Each stroke should be one action and this can be confused by moving up and down the pot.

6

7

SHAPING

8 Use an iron kidney to refine the form's shape. Most of the cutting is done, but this will create fine detail and soft curves as you cut with a broader surface. You can also completely remove your other tool marks, if desired. Use the rib edge for sharp cutting. Utilize the curves of the kidney where relevant to enhance the form.

FINISHING

9 Just as for a flat-bottomed piece (see Turning a Flat Base, pages 102–103), a chamfered edge can make a huge difference, and you may also want to consider using a steel rib to burnish the foot if it is to be unglazed inside (see Finishes, pages 104–105).

TIP With any turned piece, you may want to consider how the surface is impacted by refining. If there is a distinct change in quality between where you have refined and where you have not, try to blend the two gently together with a rib. When removing the sausages of clay from the rim, it's a good idea to keep the pot in place by holding it in the same way that you did when attaching it to the wheel head in step 2. This will keep the pot centered. If you are very gentle, it may be possible to trim right down to the rim or blend the tool marks under where the clay sits on the wheel head. This is a dangerous operation, so be very careful if you attempt it. Once the pot is complete, lift it carefully from the wheel and sponge the rim lightly to finish it off.

8

9

TURNING A FLAT BASE

For a piece that doesn't require a foot ring, a flat base can be a nice way to finish the underside of a vessel. This treatment can also improve how it meets a surface during use. A nicely turned base can reduce the chances of scratching tables or the insides of other glazed surfaces when stacked on top of other items in a cabinet. With a fast wheel speed, follow the steps for centering and attaching a pot in Turning to Create a Foot Ring (see pages 95-97). Then use a broad tool to cut away the marks left by the small tool. Then repeat step 3 of Turning to Create a Foot Ring, including the body and hand positions, but use the broader side of the tool. Start from the center of the base and work outward to the 4 o'clock position. If there is a lot of clay to remove from the side of the pot, or you have a specific profile to follow, you may want to use a small looped tool first. To flatten off the base of a cylinder, like the one shown here, turn the tool over, so it is now vertical and place it against the side of the pot. Start from the top of the side and, with a fast wheel speed, work down the pot to remove excess clay and shape the outside to the desired proportions.

TIP These techniques for turning a foot ring and turning a flat base work well for standard forms. However, if you want to turn the base of something unusual, such as a large bowl with a very fine rim, an item with a rim that isn't straight, or a bottle with a fine neck, then you will have to get creative. If you don't want the rim of something like a large bowl to touch the wheel head, you may want to consider throwing a centered mound of clay. This is a mound of clay that's tall enough to support your pot from the inside so that your piece sits on the clay and the rim is off the wheel head. The mound should be made of soft leather-hard clay, which is mildly "sticky" and can hold your pot in place for turning. For long-necked forms, you may want to consider turning in a thrown "cup." It looks like an elongated donut, and the neck of the pot can fit inside the cup. The weight of the piece is supported on its shoulder or belly by the cup. The clay used for the cup should be the same consistency as the clay used for the centered mound.

RIGHT A wide looped turning tool is used to turn the side of a cylinder.

FINISHES

Here are two ways to finish a pot after the main bulk of turning has been done. Both techniques can be applied to any and all turned pieces.

CHAMFERED EDGE

With a flat base pot, carve a slight angle between the base and the wall using the flat edge of a metal kidney. This has both an aesthetic effect and a practical purpose. When the pot is turned over, this angle will disappear under the pot, leaving just a hint of a shadow. This makes the pot feel lighter as if it is floating on a table—a feature known as a "shadow gap"—and is employed all the time by architects. On the practical side, this edge leaves a perfect line for cleaning glaze off the pot when decorating. Also, if the glaze runs a little during firing, it has a little extra surface area to cover before running onto the kiln shelf and getting the piece stuck to the shelf irreparably. It's a tiny detail, but one that can make all the difference.

BURNISHING

For any area of a pot that will be unglazed, you may want to consider burnishing. This process closes up the clay surface and gives it a slight sheen. I find it particularly nice on the unglazed underside of a pot because it hides the marks made by the throwing process and has a finished look of its own. To burnish, use a stainless-steel kidney, which has a very fine edge. When used face-on, it can polish the surface of the clay. It is worth noting here that too much burnishing can reduce the ability of glaze to adhere to the clay's surface, so be sure to only burnish where necessary. Simply hold the rib almost face-to-face with the clay surface, apply pressure to the tip, and allow the wheel to do the work. As the pot spins, the clay should become shiny.

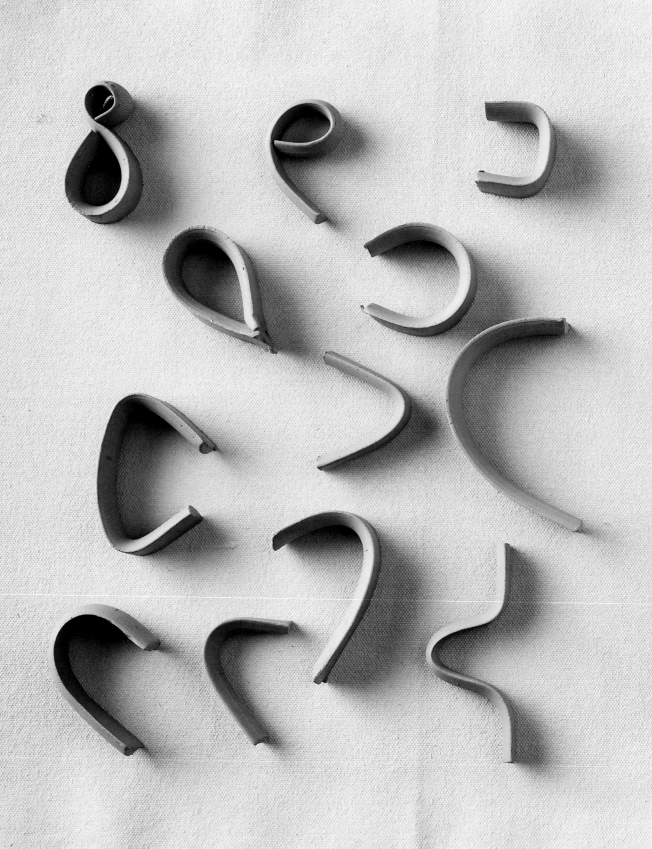

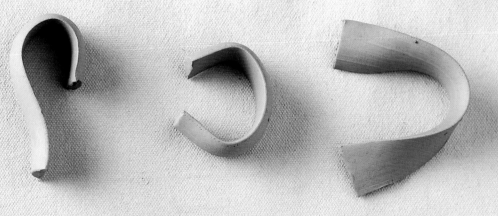

HANDLES

Handles are a functional asset to many forms of pottery, most notably cups and pitchers. While they are very common and often overlooked, there are a multitude of considerations that can make or break the success of how they look, feel, and work.

A handle needs to be fit for its functional purpose. It should be strong enough to hold the weight of both the pottery and its contents, and thick and robust enough to withstand carrying and pouring without breaking or failing off for the piece's lifespan. Alongside these, there are visual considerations; the shape, curves, joins, seams, and edges all have to complement the piece's overall form. Finally, the pot needs to feel right in the hand when used. The handle needs to be positioned so the center of gravity of the pot allows you to pour something easily. It must have graspable planes, so it doesn't slide in your hand, and be thick enough to grip with no sharp edges. All of a sudden, a handle becomes a lot more complicated. Not only does it become a piece

in its own right, but it also has to work with the design of what it's accompanying. A handle can't just be an afterthought. Any good design starts with a plan for the body of the piece and the handle, so they inform each other, rather than leading with the body and then retro-fitting a handle.

There are many ways of making handles, from pulling to pressing to casting. Here, I've decided to concentrate on three processes: roll and flatten, pulling, and extruding. I've chosen these techniques because they most closely marry the techniques we've learned so far and follow the hands-on approach I use in my own practice. Consider the style of your pot before choosing a handle technique and what qualities will enhance the overall form.

ROLL AND FLATTEN

Not all handles have to be "perfect."
Sometimes a handmade aesthetic can be very
satisfying. Here, I demonstrate how to create
a handle using a very simple technique that
can produce interesting results.

1 Form a lump of wedged clay into a sausage
by shaping it between your hands. Lay the
clay on a table and, with one hand only, start
rolling it out into a long coil. If the clay starts
to become a little square, pick it up and give it
a twist from opposite ends. This should help
the coil become more round as you continue
to roll. It's a good idea to roll a long coil from
which you can cut multiple handles.

Once the coil reaches the desired length,
pick it up from its ends and firmly, but in a
considered way, slap it down onto the work
surface. Now, with one side flattened, pick up
the coil and carefully lay it out on a thin cloth
or newspaper. Align the edge against a stick
or ruler to make it straight.

2 Take a very slightly damp sponge and run it
along the length of the curved side of the coil,
smoothing it out and evening out any lumps
and bumps.

3 Cut the coil into pieces in the desired length
of your handles. Consider cutting at an angle
if it will help attach the handles later. Roughly
shape the handles to your chosen form and
let them dry to the soft-leather stage for
attaching.

1

2

PULLING

This involves working a lump of clay with a wet hand so it begins to stretch and elongate.

1 Form a torpedo-shaped lump of wedged clay—using clay on the slightly firmer side is best. Make sure to have plenty of clay for all the handles you want to make. Grip the clay from one end. I find that patting the top flat over the thumb and index finger of the left hand helps it stay in place without needing to grip it too tightly for a long period, as this can be tiring and hard on the joints. Keep a bowl of water handy or work over the sink, as this can be a messy job. Dip your right hand in the water and grip the narrow end of the clay. Move your hand up and down along the tube. Keep turning your hand back and forth at the wrist to even the action all the way around and start pulling the clay down with your left hand into a rough tube.

2 As you feel the clay start to get longer, begin moving your hand downward only. Be careful to adjust the pressure as the clay becomes thinner so you do not pull the end off. Keep your hand just wet enough to avoid creating friction against the clay at all times. Try to keep the length evenly tapered so the hanging end is the narrowest and the top end is the thickest. If the clay becomes too thin, simply cut that section off and start again higher up on the tube.

1

2

3 Once the clay starts to reach the desired length for the handle, begin considering its profile. By repeatedly running your hand down its length, with your fingers shaped as if you are gripping a handle, you can alter the profile to one that's very comfortable to hold. Run your thumb down the clay. This will create a plane, which forms an easy-to-grip handle. This adds stability and comfort for pouring, but, although comfortable, it may not be essential in items such as cups where the gripping action is different. A general rule is that the edge of a handle should mirror the edge of the pot's rim in terms of thickness and finish. The handle can, however, retain thickness in the middle for strength.

4 Once you have the handle as you want it, cut the clay off about 1 inch (2.5 cm) higher than you require. Hold the handle from this excess section and use it as a stand as you turn the handle upside down. This will allow the handle to curve while it dries. It also forms a very natural curve, as it hasn't been manipulated into shape. Once the handle has dried to soft leather, the ends can be cut appropriately for attaching. For longer handles, it is common to hang the length from a shelf or off the edge of a table until it dries enough to be shaped. In this case, be sure to stick it down to the surface well so that it can't drop off.

3

4

EXTRUDING

Extruding is a quick and accurate way of producing consistent handles. It requires an extruder, which, in simple terms, is a solid container into which clay can be loaded. The extruder has a plunger that squashes the clay through the body and out through a die plate. A die plate is a solid, flat form made to fit the end of the extruder and has a profile through which the clay is pushed. An extruder can also be used for making coils for hand building, belts, or details for decoration, and more advanced models can even create hollow tubes of varying shapes and sizes.

I have made my own die plates for my handles. The profile of the handle has a curved side designed to sit comfortably in the fingers and a flat side for gripping with the thumb. This profile also allows the handle to be moderately thick, giving it strength, and a fine edge that gives it a delicate appearance. I have different sizes of the same profile for different-sized pots: small for coffee cups, medium for mugs, and large for pitchers. Most new extruders come with a set of standard die plates.

I use a large, wall-mounted extruder, also known as a wad box, but you can get handheld versions as small as a sealant gun from most good pottery suppliers.

1 Prepare some wedged clay to fit into the body of your extruder. Secure the die plate in place and compress the plunger to squeeze out a length of clay in your handle profile.

2 Lay the extrusions out on an appropriately sized board, with a layer of newspaper between the clay and the board. Line the first extrusion up against a straight stick or ruler, and then use that as a line to place the remaining extrusions parallel to each other. This way, you can make lots of handles at once. For your first handle, cut multiple sizes from one length to test against your pot to figure out a standard size that works. Then measure and mark that length across the extrusions and carefully cut through them all, supporting them with your hand so they don't warp when cutting. Consider cutting at an angle if it will help attach them later. Shape the handles to your chosen form and let them dry to the soft-leather stage for attaching to the vessel.

ATTACHING

Positioning and attaching a handle correctly are vital to the function and durability of a piece. There are several different ways of attaching a handle. However, they all serve the same purpose: to secure the handle to the body. Here, I demonstrate a few options for joining.

Lining up and marking the handle's position is an important step before sticking it to the pot. This stage gives you the chance to try the handle in different positions on the body of the piece. Once satisfied, make a small mark at the top and bottom of the body with a knife or pin. These will serve as the guide marks for attaching.

SMALL AND FINE HANDLES

1 Sometimes simple is better. When working with fine, thin-walled pots and small handles, just water is often enough to join the handle. This works best with less groggy clay like fine stoneware or porcelain. Simply start by dipping the ends of the handle in water.

2 Carefully put the handle in position and push it firmly against the wall of the pot, supporting the body from the inside with your free hand so you don't distort the form. Be sure there are no gaps in the seam. Allow the seam to dry off a little as the water is absorbed into the clay and then smooth edges where possible with a finger.

3 Use a small, damp paintbrush to blend the joins all the way around and then finish with a little sponging. This join is delicate and will require a covering of glaze in the decoration stage. The glaze will fuse the surface like a layer of glue, making the handle nice and strong.

1

2

3

1

WIDER AND THICKER HANDLES

1 For a larger join with a slightly thicker pot, you will need to adopt a technique known as scoring and slipping. The idea here is to score the surface of the join on both the handle and the pot with crosshatched marks and use slip (a wet clay that has a heavy-cream consistency, see page124) as a cement to bond the two sections. Use the marks you made at the start as reference points for where to score and scratch the surface so it is well roughed up. Make lots and lots of marks in varying directions, not just a few crosses. Do the same to the end of the handle.

2

3

4

2 Apply a healthy smear of slip to the ends of the handle and push it into place on the side of the pot. Make sure not to leave any gaps and support the pot from the inside while you push. Do not remove the excess slip at this stage. Let it dry for half an hour or so.

3 After some time, the moisture from the slip will be absorbed into the clay and it will firm up to a similar state to that of the pot and handle. Use your finger and modeling tools to blend the seams. Try to push the stiff slip into the join rather than cut it away. This will compress the seam and make the join very strong.

4 Use a slightly damp sponge and paintbrush to smooth over the joins and make a seamless juncture between the pot and handle.

THICK AND CHUNKY HANDLES
This works particularly well for pulled handles as you can control the varied thickness in the handle, leaving it chunky enough to blend into the surface.

1 To attach the handle, follow the scoring and slipping method shown on pages 116–117, but use slightly less slip.

2 Push the handle firmly against the body, supporting the wall from the inside with your free hand if necessary.

1

2

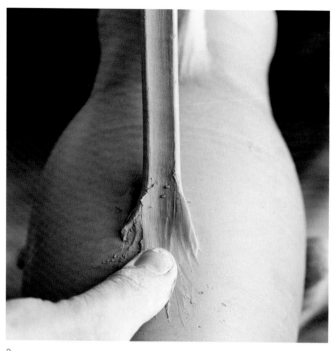

3

4

3 Remove any excess slip and mold the handle into the body of the pot. If you prefer the look of the finger molding, you may wish to keep it or even exaggerate it around the seam.

4 To soften and blend the join between the pot and the handle, rub with a slightly damp sponge. The more you clean up, the less the join will show, but be careful not to take them out completely if the marks add to the form.

5 It is often worth turning the pot upside down while it is drying. Gravity will stop the handle from slumping. Drying in this way also makes the handle feel as if it has a "spring" when it is turned the right way up and becomes firm.

5

CHAPTER 4

DECORATION—GLAZING AND FIRING

SURFACE FINISHES

Surface finishes are as wide-ranging as the forms in ceramics, and the creative possibilities are endless. Here, I explore some of the most common techniques, but it is important to see them as a starting point to the fascinating discoveries that also result from firing.

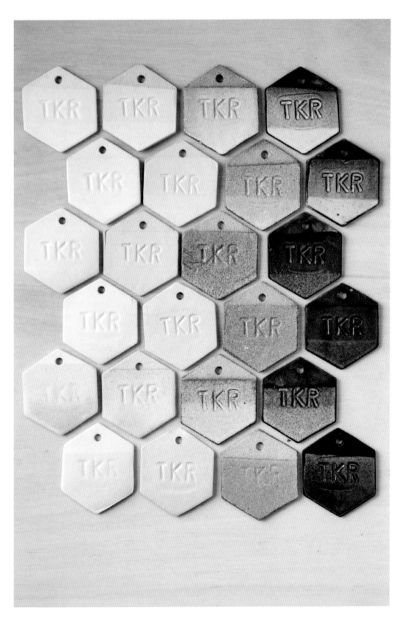

For the purposes of this section, I used pots that had a first firing to 1,742°F (950°C). This is known as a biscuit or bisque firing and changes the state of the pot from clay to ceramic. The change happens at around 1,112°F (600°C). The higher you fire clay, the less porous it will be. 1,742–1,832°F (950–1,000°C) is a good bisque temperature for stoneware because the pot is fairly strong and can withstand being handled, but is still porous enough to suck glaze into its surface. I then fired the piece to 2,300°F (1,260°C), which is a medium temperature for stoneware glazes.

The surface of a pot is much like a blank canvas with three dimensions. You also have the added challenges of controlling the temperature in the kiln, the melting points of glaze, and the boiling points of clay. It can be a minefield, but also a joyful exploration as you experiment and learn what different materials do and how and when to use them effectively.

Most beginners in pottery tend to shy away from glazing and regard it as an afterthought, as they're so caught up in the messy fun of making the form. However, it's a mistake not to think about the glazing until the end, even though this is the final process. Surface finishes should be a consideration at the planning stage, so that the final surface can inform the making process and vice versa. Try to think of a glaze or decorated surface as a nice outfit—you want something that goes with your form, complements your body, sits well with your skin tone, and shows off your sense of style. You don't want to wear something that just happens to be lying around and that you hope will fit!

Another reason I think people are slow on the uptake with glaze and decoration is the technical aspects. I, for one, spent years not engaging with the process for fear of doing something wrong. It boils down to confidence. Confidence comes with knowledge and knowledge comes with time, so engage with decoration right from the start and make it part of the learning process. With just a few helpful starting points gleaned from this chapter, I hope you'll be able to start learning and building your confidence.

Just as in painting or drawing, a blank page can be daunting. If there's one thing I've learned from ten years in arts education, it's that nobody "can't draw or paint." It's just that our perception of what drawing and painting means is skewed. Just by getting to this stage of the process, you have drawn something, only you have used clay rather than a pencil (although, hopefully, you used a pencil when planning the design of your piece). Ceramics can be a wonderful medium through which to explore your artistic ability and has a bit of something for everyone. For the technically minded, there is a world of detail and knowledge to acquire, materials to try, and uses to learn. For the sleek and chic, you can make one glaze and only alter its color and tone. You can base your choices on this season's fashion or your latest hair color. And for the explorers, there is a world of different colors and ready-made glazes to discover—you really can try them all.

LEFT Glazed test tiles. The rows show different glazes; the columns show different clays.

DECORATING SLIP

Slip is wet clay—literally clay mixed with water. Slips become part of the clay body and can be glazed over or left bare. As we've seen, it can be used to attach handles to pieces. It can also be used as a decorating base. However, it is usual to mix decorating slip with slightly finer materials. Since decorating slip is made of clay, it will retain a texture and thickness after firing. Mixing your own slip means working with dry materials (see Mixing and Sieving, page 136), which is ideal because you can work out accurate measurements and repeat the results. Slip must be applied at the clay stage before any firings. The clay should be leather-hard or softer. Remember, however, that using a lot of wet slip can saturate a pot, so be careful not to add too much at the wrong stage.

ABOVE Slip tests showing (from top to bottom) cream, yellow, green, blue, and brown. The tiles are made with (from left to right) porcelain, white stoneware, crank, and black clay.

BASE SLIP FOR STONEWARE CLAY

The base recipe is usually written out as parts of 100 with a color addition. For instance, if you're aiming for 35 ounces (1 kg) of slip, that would be:

17½ ounces (500 g) ball clay
17½ ounces (500 g) china clay
Add 1 ounce (30 g) copper carbonate

This makes 36 ounces (1,030 g), which is slightly more than is needed. However, this approach keeps things simple. As long as you get the desired results, it's fine to have recipes like these. Potters usually try to balance recipes out to 100 percent, but sometimes, with additions such as oxides or stains, it's just easier to fudge the math. Most potters rely on trial and error using test tiles.

Here are my favorite recipes.

CREAM
50 ball clay
50 china clay

YELLOW
50 ball clay
50 china clay
Add 4 yellow stain

GREEN
50 ball clay
50 china clay
Add 3 copper carbonate (copper makes green in electric firing)

BLUE
50 ball clay
50 china clay
Add 1.5 cobalt oxide

BROWN
50 ball clay
50 china clay
Add 5 iron oxide

SLIP APPLICATION

Slip can be applied in many ways. Think of it like paint. Colors can be mixed together and tend to be opaque where they are applied in several layers.

1 TRAILING

This traditional decorating technique uses a bulb or slip trailer. It's similar to piping a cake with a frosting bag, and, if your slip is just the right consistency, you can even use piping tools to create interesting textures. Here, I used a syringe without a needle. I like the control this gives and find it slightly less messy than other more common tools. I use slip with a heavy-cream consistency so it can move freely through the nozzle and hold its shape without running or bleeding. This technique is traditionally used for fast-line drawings, mainly of animals. With practice, it is possible to make very fluid and confident marks.

2 FEATHERING

Using runny slips, pour on a base layer and then build up your decorations with drops or lines. Run a pointed tool through the slips to drag them out into interesting patterns.

3 SGRAFFITO AND INLAY

Sgraffito is the process of scratching through layers of slip to draw a pattern. It can also be useful in combination with painting, as you can highlight fine details using the tip of a pin. If done carefully, it is possible to scratch through a layer at a time, revealing colors below the top surface. This can be done with a metal kidney for larger areas. Inlay is more or less the opposite technique to sgraffito. Here, the pattern is drawn first and then filled over with slip. Let the slip dry and scrape the surface back, leaving only the slip used to create the detail.

4 MARBLING

Using slips with a runny consistency, pour on a base color, then drop in some of another. Move the clay around so the slips run into each other, forming a marbled effect.

5 STENCILING AND SPONGING

Stencils cut from masking tape or newspaper can be used to cover areas to protect them after layering colors. When painting with slips, it's a good idea to do about three layers to ensure the result is opaque. Apply the slip thinner in layers where you want a washy effect. Here, I've torn shapes from newspaper—making them wet helps them stay in place. Each time you lay a shape down, block out the color for that layer. Use a blow-dryer to dry the slip between coats and layers. Stencils turn white when dry, making it easier to locate and remove them. On top of this, I've used a cut sponge stuck to a handle to dip in slip and stamp a shape. Spongeware, as it is known, has a rich history as a decorative technique.

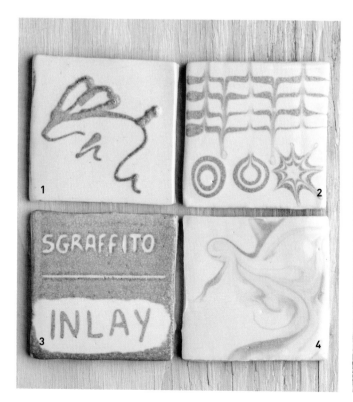

OXIDES

Oxides are strong natural colorants for clays and glazes. They can be added to clay bodies, as well as slip and glaze recipes. They have a high heat tolerance, which is perfect for stoneware firing temperatures. You can also use them as decorative pigments by mixing with water or another medium and applying under or onto glaze. When applying before the glaze, it is possible to transfer some oxide into a glaze and contaminate a batch. For this reason, I always paint on top of freshly glazed surfaces. You must, however, be careful when loading the kiln because if you get oxide on your gloved fingertips, it's easily transferred to other pots.

Oxides are essentially oxidized metals that are ground down into powder form. One easy-to-understand example is iron oxide. Oxidized iron is basically rust, something we're all familiar with. It is reddish-brown and fires to a similar color.

Oxides can be very dangerous to health, and caution should be taken not to inhale, ingest, or have direct skin contact with oxide (see Mixing and Sieving, pages 136–137).

Most oxides will change from a pale hue to a strong color to black and metallic depending on the thickness of the application. Below are a few examples applied on top of a freshly glazed test cylinder and how they look when fired to 2,300°F (1,260°C).

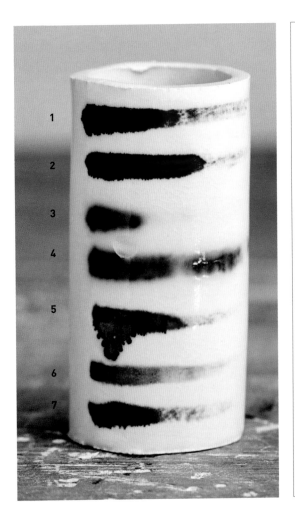

1 COBALT OXIDE
Very strong dark blue

2 COBALT CARBONATE
Strong blue (pink/purple flecks in some glazes)

3 COPPER OXIDE
Strong green; tends to create a slight green halo

4 COPPER CARBONATE
Strong green (paler than oxide in some slips and glazes)

5 MANGANESE DIOXIDE
Yellowish-brown to black; runny on glossy glazes

6 IRON OXIDE
Brown, consistent, and stable

7 BLACK IRON OXIDE
Brown/black; more metallic; can bleed on glossy glazes

UNDERGLAZES

Underglazes are ready-made coloring materials. Most are branded, and companies won't give the recipes away. It's fair to assume that they include an amount of oxide or other natural or man-made colorants combined with a tiny amount of clay to give them some body. They also often come with a "binder" addition. Binder makes them more sticky, to ensure they don't dry too quickly on absorbent, low-fired ceramics, and can adhere to the surface, and set a little harder when dry—all useful at the decorating stage. Some underglazes can be used directly on the clay before firing, but it is probably most common to use them after the first firing when the pot is more stable and handleable. They are called underglazes because they are usually applied before a glaze. The glaze will cover them, seal the surface, and also deepen their tone. You can use underglaze without a covering of glaze so that the clay body is covered but remains a "dry" surface. This will work better with certain manufacturers, and the clay you're using can have an influence too—testing is always advisable here (see page 138).

When purchased in dry form, underglazes can be used to color clay bodies and glazes (usually in a 1 to 6 percent ratio). Technically, body stains are the best choices for this, but the two are very similar and often interchangeable. A "stain" will probably have no binder, making it easier to combine, but I've rarely found a great difference when using dry materials. A dry underglaze is usually simply mixed with water to the desired consistency if you are using it as a decorative "paint" (for more guidance on additions in glazes, see page 134).

LEFT Some examples of ready-made underglazes bought in liquid form and applied under a transparent glaze after a first firing to 1,740°F/ 950°C.

COLOR

As you start learning about which materials do what, it's really easy to be led by what you know you can do rather than what you want to do.

For example, if I know that I want to make a blue pot and I know cobalt gives me blue, that's a good starting point. But cobalt is a specific blue—is that really the shade I want? If not, then I need to think of a new approach to create what I want before I slap on the wrong color. This way of thinking can slow the process down a little, but it means you're making deliberate choices rather than being led by what's easy to make. Testing and record-keeping is imperative to learning how to decorate in a thoughtful and practical way. Consider color from the perspective of a designer with no material knowledge. They simply choose a color because it looks good on the form, not because they know how to make it. That should be your starting point. If, after testing, the color proves difficult to create, or the right tone is elusive, only then think about what you can create. If you're close enough to having a nice color, perhaps try it out on a prototype and let this reinform the design so that the two are harmonious again.

LEFT Thrown tableware glazed in muted colors with a satin finish.

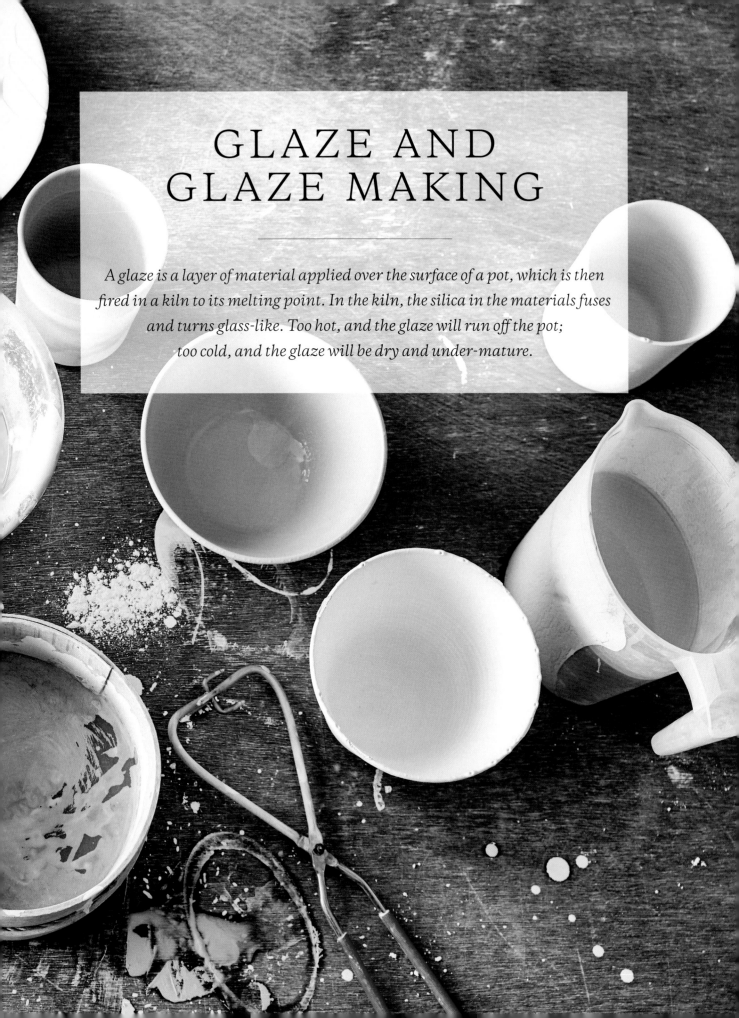

GLAZE AND GLAZE MAKING

A glaze is a layer of material applied over the surface of a pot, which is then fired in a kiln to its melting point. In the kiln, the silica in the materials fuses and turns glass-like. Too hot, and the glaze will run off the pot; too cold, and the glaze will be dry and under-mature.

Choosing the right glaze is as important as choosing what to make. There are lots of considerations when making your selection. Is the glaze food-safe? Does it fit the body properly? How does it look? How does it feel? How glossy or matte should it be? The list goes on and on. I advise you to start with what look you want, consider the color and qualities you're looking for, and then find a ready-made glaze or glaze recipe to match. Try not to just consider what materials you have, and pick the best of what's available. This involves more work, but once you have a recipe that works, it's yours for life.

Glaze has two main functions in ceramics: one is aesthetic—it should complement the form like a well-tailored suit does a person's body. The other is a practical one: an unglazed surface is dry and tends to be a bit rough, if only on a microscopic level. Glaze provides a slick closed surface that is ideal for function; a closed surface leaves little opportunity for stains or bacteria to build up on household wares. Glazed items are easily cleaned and dry quickly, which are both positives for daily use.

The idea of making glazes from scratch is daunting, even for experienced professionals, but it doesn't have to be. There is a wealth of information on glazes and available materials. Though there are more details than we have space for here, I want to demystify the process a little and give you the tools to start your own investigations. It's worth noting at this point that it is possible to "raw-glaze" pots, which means glazing them before a firing and only firing once.

Personally, I find this process to be fraught with problems and highly recommend doing a bisque firing first to around 1,742°F (950°C). This will make the pot strong enough for handling and porous enough to suck the glaze into the surface.

Firstly, you need to understand what a glaze recipe is and how it works. A glaze recipe is a combination of materials that gives a specific result. Let's take baking a cake as an example of how to build a recipe. Most cakes use similar ingredients that appear in lots of recipes, but some use very different ingredients that you may not have heard of but that are usually available from good retailers. It's the same with glaze materials. Let's say you'd like to make a lemon cake. Now, in order to start, we need to know the ingredients for a plain cake. Look at this as a "base recipe." If you want to flavor the cake, you're going to need an additional ingredient, such as chocolate or vanilla. You will need different quantities of these additions because their potency varies. To determine this quantity, I'm going to look at other cakes and see how much lemon they use as

TOP Glaze making tools, including a scoop, stirrer, sticks, bowls, sponge, and sieve.

BELOW Stirrer and sticks for mixing glaze.

flavoring. In some, the lemon flavor is barely there, while others are too sharp. But one is very similar to what I want, so I'll test a small bit of my recipe with that amount of lemon. If it's too much or too little, I'll adjust the recipe and test again before I bake a whole batch. During this testing, I'll also look for some advice on how hot the oven should be and how long the sponge should be baked for. By adjusting the baking time, I can vary the results. Choosing the quantity of a coloring addition for glaze works just like determining the amount of lemon flavoring for a cake. It involves testing and some trial-and-error. This sums up the firing process pretty well, too. As you get to know your recipe, ingredients, and kiln, you'll be able to tweak the process over time to get the best results.

There is one other consideration. Think of your pot as the baking pan. You have to be sure that it's designed to go to the same temperature as the cake. This is easy to find out as it's written on the packaging of the pan (or clay). If you send a plastic pan into an oven, it's going to melt. The same can be said of taking a low-temperature clay to a high-temperature glaze firing—it's simply not made for that. That's not to say the tray with the lower melting point isn't useful, just that it can only be used for cakes that don't require heat. For a 2,300°F (1,260°C) glaze, like the one I'll be using in the following examples, you'll need a stoneware clay (the metal baking pan in the example). The plastic tray in this analogy is earthenware clay and that usually only fires to about 1,940°F (1,060°C). I tend to use stoneware or porcelain in my practice, which is why I'm sticking to them for the examples here. However, there is a world of information, examples, and recipes available for other clays in most glaze books.

LEFT Thrown tableware fired to 2300°F (1260°C) with satin glazes.

GLAZE RECIPES

Here are three base recipes that you can try yourself. They all fire to 2,300°F (1,260°C). However, temperatures that are a little higher or lower (50°F/10°C each way) will produce slightly different results—the glaze will usually be glossier at a higher temperature and more matte at a lower one. For each base, I've also provided an example with a color addition, alternating between stains and oxides, so you get an idea of how they work and what they do in a base recipe.

The amounts in the base recipe are written out as parts of 100. Often, a recipe will add up to more than 100 when you include the color addition. Try not to worry too much—just add the amount and allow the recipe to be over—as long as you get the desired results, there are no hard-and-fast rules.

1 BRILLIANT WHITE BASE
Bright white, opaque, flat satin finish; food-safe.
45 potash feldspar
22 dolomite
16 quartz
11 zirconium silicate
6 china clay

1a BRILLIANT WHITE BASE WITH LEMON
Yellow with small iron fleck, opaque, flat satin finish; food-safe.
Add 3 canary-yellow stain
Add 1 iron oxide

2 MATTE TRANSPARENT BASE
Shows clay body color; some broad crazing; buttery matte finish; food-safe, though food may stain crazing.
39 potash feldspar
20 whiting
25 china clay
16 flint

2a MATT TRANSPARENT BASE WITH SATIN GREEN / BLACK
Dark black when thin, mottled moss green when thick; opaque, satin sheen finish; food-safe.
Add 4 nickel

Add 5 red iron oxide
Add 1.5 cobalt carbonate

3 GLOSS CRACKLE BASE
Shows clay body color; highly crazed surface; high-gloss finish; food-safe, though food may stain the crazing.
64 Cornish stone (or substitute)
18 whiting
6 china clay
6 dolomite
6 flint

3a GLOSS CRACKLE BASE WITH PEAL BLUE
Soft electric celadon green; transparent; highly crazed surface; high-gloss finish; food-safe, though food may stain crazing.
Add 0.2 copper oxide

BASIC ADJUSTMENTS
Common terms used to discuss materials are flux and matting agents. A flux is a substance that melts well whereas a matting agent is a substance that doesn't. For example, quartz is a flux, and dolomite and china clay are matting agents. If you want your glaze to be glossy, increase the flux and reduce the matting agent; if you want it to be rigid and matte, reduce the flux and increase the matting agent.

MIXING AND SIEVING

Mixing a glaze is time-consuming, but it is a simple process. The steps are very easy: weigh the materials and add them to a pail, sieving to remove any impurities from the mix and to combine the fine particles, particularly those of color additions, so they are evenly distributed throughout the glaze.

1 To make a glaze, measure out the materials with a scale and place them in a pail. Use a recipe to work out the quantities you need. For example, if you want to mix 90 ounces (3 kg) of glaze and your recipe is roughly in parts of 100, you'll need to multiply each part by 0.9, so 50 potash x 0.9 = 45 ounces/1,500 g potash. For small additions or test batches, you may need a jeweler's scale that allows you to measure the weight to one-tenth of a gram; these can be found online for very little money.

Once you have all the materials together, cover with water and stir. I suggest stirring with a stick until the ingredients are well mixed. You should avoid skin contact with

NOTE When you are working with any dry materials in ceramics, it is imperative that you protect yourself from the dangerous effects of silica dust. Silica is found in all ceramic materials, and when released as dust, it enters the lungs and never leaves. The effects are cumulative and, while a little here and there may not seem much, over years of practice it can add up to fatal levels and cause a disease known as silicosis or "potter's lung." You must wear a mask that covers your nose and mouth, and it should ideally have a rubber-molded form to ensure there are no gaps. The filter on the mask needs to have a rating of P3. No other filter is small enough to catch the minute silica particles, so don't throw on any old paper dust mask and think you're protecting yourself. Where possible, work in an area with good ventilation, or outside, when you are dealing with dry materials.

1

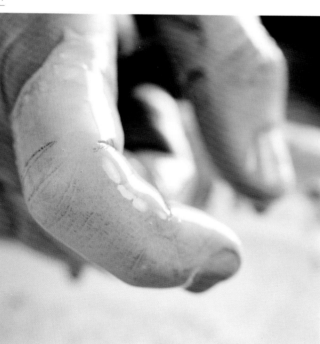

2

3

oxides until they are diluted in the glaze mixture. If you are at all concerned, or if you're working with large quantities, I recommend wearing gloves. Make sure to have enough water in the mix so it is fluid, somewhere between milk and light-cream consistency, and mixed smooth.

2 Place two sticks over the empty pail, parallel to each other. Balance a glaze sieve on the sticks over the empty pail and pour the glaze mixture through until the sieve is almost full. I usually use a bottle brush to stir the glaze and push it through the sieve. Keep topping up the sieve until all the contents pass through. Repeat this step with a finer sieve. I use a 60 mesh sieve followed by a 120. The higher the number, the finer the holes. A 120 mesh sieve is perfect for the recipes in this chapter. Once the glaze is sieved, allow it to settle for a few hours or overnight, then pour off the excess water and stir.

3 Add water back into the mixture until it reaches your desired consistency. I usually aim for a glaze consistency that covers the skin of the hand, but breaks on the knuckles.

TESTING

It's vitally important that you test glazes on a small scale before sending your work to the kiln. If the glaze is runny and you're making upright forms, it's advisable to test on something fired upright, so you get a good idea of how the glaze will move. If you're making flat items, such as plates, or using a very static glaze, it's fine to test on a small flat tile. When testing a new glaze with a color, it's good practice to produce a line blend (see the next section).

LINE BLEND

A line blend is a group of tests using the same glaze base and increasing the quantities of color addition to create different samples. I suggest five tests with color additions percentages increasing from 1 to 5 percent, using one tile for each test. When using cobalt, I decrease the percentages of the color addition by 0.5 percent for each test, as the cobalt is very strong. The following basic line blend gives a good idea of the typical process.

BASIC LINE BLEND

Mix and sieve 3 ounces (100 g) of glaze. Dip one tile (this is a base test). Next add 1 percent of your color addition, sieve, and dip another tile. Repeat until you reach 5 percent of the color addition. Mark each tile with an underglaze pencil or some iron oxide and water, so you can identify them, although it should be fairly obvious from the color addition of the glaze. Each time you dip, you remove some of the mixture, which makes color additions difficult to monitor. That's why I always suggest a final test with accurate measurements based on the results of the line blend.

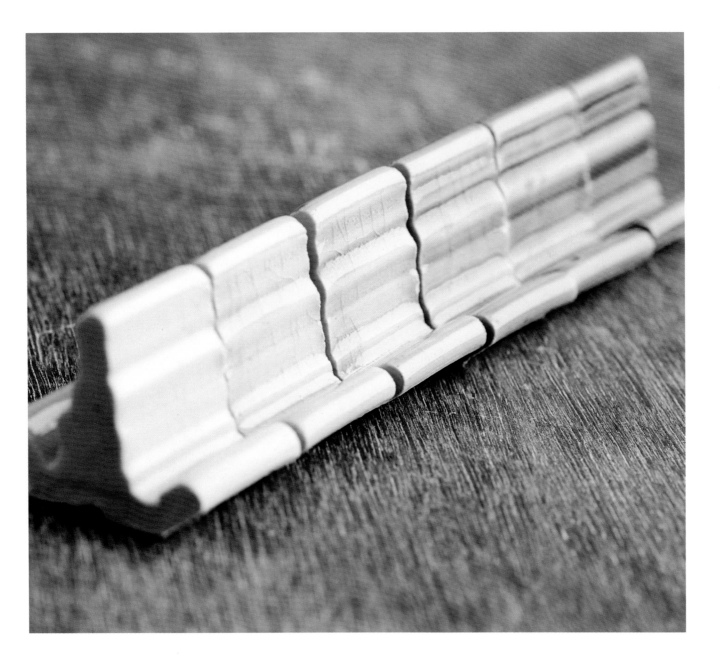

APPLICATION

There are many ways of applying glaze, from brushing to more traditional pouring and dipping techniques. You'll need to adapt these techniques to suit your pot and chosen glaze.

DIPPING BY HAND

1 Place a finger on the base of the pot and a thumb on the rim to hold the pot. Submerge the whole pot. Hold the pot upright under the surface of the glaze. As you remove the pot, turn it over so that it is upside down when it emerges from the glaze. Gently roll the pot in your hand so any drips around the rim keep moving until they dry. The porosity of the pot is sufficient to absorb the moisture from the glaze in a few seconds, leaving a dry surface. Place the pot down on its base.

2 Dip a finger in the glaze so that a drip forms on your fingertip. Touch the drip to the area that was masked by your thumb, to fill in the space. Once the pot has dried, you can rub down or gently scrape the rim a little to blend the surface. If you do this later, when the glaze is very dry, wear a mask to protect yourself from the dust.

3 To dip a plate (or wide dish), decant the glaze into a wide bowl. Hold the piece at the rim with two or three fingers on each side. Dip the piece into the glaze, from the front of the bowl and out through the back. Hold the middle down for a second or two, to ensure a good coat of glaze. Lift the plate out and hold it up to face your body, then roll it from side to side like a steering wheel so the drips run around the rim. Touch up the finger marks, as you did in step 2.

4 To dip the outside of a pot only (which is usually done in combination with a poured inside), hold it from the inside with the fingers of each hand. Carefully dip the pot upright into the glaze and try to cover the rim without glaze pouring into the pot.

TIP Always stir the glaze well before dipping. Materials can settle quickly, so always mix the glaze after you've dipped a pot to avoid saturating it with a water layer that has separated from the other materials. When dipping each pot, work to a beat of three to time the duration it sits in the glaze. Here's the rhythm: in, 2, 3, and out.

1
—

2
—

3
—

4
—

DIPPING WITH TONGS

Follow the technique for Dipping by Hand (see page 140), but hold the pot with glazing tongs in its thickest area (usually toward the base). Once the pot is dry, put it down and rub over the tong marks with a finger. They should disappear when the glaze melts in the kiln.

POURING

1 For the inside of a pot, pour in the glaze to fill the pot two-thirds of the way up. Turn the pot over a pail to pour out the glaze. Rotate the pot in your hands so that the glaze covers the rest of the inside as it is poured out. Try to go around twice. Clean away any dribbles with a damp sponge. Allow the pot to dry well before applying the outside layer.

2 Pouring glazes on the outside of a pot requires setting up some equipment. Place a bowl on a banding wheel, put two sticks over the bowl, and balance the upturned rim of the pot on top. Take a pitcher of glaze and, while spinning the pot and bowl with one hand, pour the glaze from the foot of the pot over the surface. Try to rotate fully twice while pouring. Once the pot is touch-dry, pick it up and fill in any gaps made by the sticks, as in step 2 of Dipping by Hand (see page 140).

1

2

SPRAYING

Spray glazing is an art in its own right. Always spray glaze in a well-ventilated room with good air extraction and, ideally, in a spray booth. You'll need a good compressor and a gravity-fed spray gun. You must learn and test how to get the best results from your gun by adjusting the airflow, spray width, and volume of glaze that it can spray. Fill the gun container with glaze and place the pot upside down on top of something narrower and taller than your piece, such as a cylinder. This ensures the pot is supported from the inside and the rim is hovering. The support should be centered on a banding wheel. Spinning the wheel with one hand, start spraying at the base of the pot and work down toward the rim. This action should be controlled so that you apply enough glaze to the body of the pot without causing drips. Practice doing this quickly rather than building up in layers, as this can leave an unwanted texture in the glaze surface.

Turn the pot the right side up and center it on the banding wheel. While spinning the wheel again, begin to spray from the internal base up to the rim. Be aware that, as a pot gets wider, you have a broader surface to cover. You will need to be quick in the narrow areas to avoid overglazing and slower in wider areas to avoid thin patches.

NOTE You must clean the glaze from the base and also a fraction up the sides to account for glaze that runs when firing. This can be done with a damp sponge. I also find a damp carpet tile useful for cleaning in a straight and consistent line. If you do not clean the base, it will fuse to the kiln shelf when the glaze melts during firing.

TOP A gravity-fed spray gun.

LEFT It is important to clean the glaze from the base of a pot to prevent it from sticking to the kiln.

FIRING

*Firing is the process of heating clay to change its state.
For stoneware clay, there are two main changes.*

At around 1,112°F (600°C), it changes from clay to ceramic—it is set hard and all of the chemically bound water is driven off, changing its nature, which means it cannot be reconstituted into clay. Between 2,192°F (1,200°C) and 2,372°F (1,300°C), most stonewares and porcelains will become vitrified. This means that even without glaze, the body is closed and impenetrable to water. Stoneware clay fired at a temperature at or above the 2,000°F (1,200°C) will shrink by between 8 and 20 percent, depending on the clay. You should test and account for this in the design process. The shrinking of the clay closes its body and makes it vitrified—imagine the particles getting closer and closer until they form bonds and become a fused unit.

There are two common fuels for studio firing: gas and electric. Other fuels such as oil and wood are used and achieve specific results, but for the purposes of this book, we will leave those specialist firings for another time. Gas firing is becoming less common, but still has appeal as you can get very different results. You can limit the airflow in a gas kiln (known as reduction), forcing the flame to burn the oxygen out of the ceramic materials. This changes their chemical formula and, in turn, their appearance. For example, in a "normal" firing, known as oxidation, in which oxygen is allowed into the kiln, copper produces green. In reduction, copper produces red. There is a whole world of reduction glazing to be explored. However, in my practice, and as a result of both health and safety and environmental concerns around the burning of gas, an electric kiln does the job nicely. For this reason, the following method is based on electric firing and oxidation.

KILNS

An electric kiln works by passing an electric current through coils of nichrome wire called elements. Every kiln has its own type of element that varies in length and number of coils. They all, however, serve the same purpose: the current produces heat that is distributed throughout the kiln and around the pots.

Modern electric kilns are operated and overseen by a device known as a controller. Through the controller, you can program how you want the kiln to fire and ensure it turns itself off at the right time. The controller tells the elements when to heat up and when to cut out. It is also connected to a pyrometer, which relays and displays the temperature in the kiln. With the controller you can enter a firing program. This dictates the end temperature, how quickly the kiln reaches that point, and for how long it stays there. I give some examples of these page 146.

Most kilns have vent holes to allow moisture and gases to escape. A kiln should be housed in a well-ventilated area, ideally with localized air extraction to avoid breathing in these gases. The vent holes should be closed at around 1,112°F (600°C). Below this temperature, it is beneficial for the life span of the kiln to allow the gases to escape; above this temperature, it is uneconomical to allow heat loss. You fill the vents with what are

known as bungs or peeks, which are made from a ceramic material and can withstand heat.

If you want to double-check that your pyrometer is reading accurately, then you can use a pyrometric cone placed inside the kiln. This small triangular cone can be held up by a little clay at the base. There are several different numbered cones, and each one has a specific melting point. If you've set your kiln to 2,300°F/1,260°C (cone 8), with cones 7, 8, and 9 inside, you would expect 7 to have melted quite flat, 8 to be well-bent, and 9 to be standing with a little curve. Cones also provide an accurate measurement for "heat work," meaning that if you have fired for a long time, they will be more glossy and perhaps more melted. Cones reflect what your pots are going through in the kiln and should be used regularly.

PACKING A KILN

When loading a kiln, potters use "kiln furniture," including shelves and props (or stilts). You build layers starting with a shelf of pots, adding taller props, then another shelf, then pots and props, and another shelf, and so on. In most kilns, it is typical to use three props per shelf. This helps the shelf balance like a tripod. The props must be positioned in the same place on each shelf so that the weight of the pots is supported. If there are raised supports in the bottom of the kiln, you can use them to position the props.

BISCUIT FIRING

All work for a bisque must be bone-dry. If it feels cold to the touch, then it may still be damp. Damp pots, or pots with trapped air bubbles, are prone to exploding in the kiln. This is because once hot, the air and moisture expand and become volatile. They need to escape quickly, which forces the pot apart, sometimes in a dramatic fashion.

Pots can touch and be stacked in a biscuit firing, as they won't stick together. However, they should not touch the elements or kiln wall. When stacking, ensure the weight of an inner pot is not held inside the rim of an outer one—as expansion and contraction take place, the pots need to be free to move a little, rims may crack. A carefully packed bisque firing can hold a huge volume of pots, and it's worth considering economical kiln usage in the design process because a small tweak may increase the volume in each firing, saving time, money, and energy.

GLAZE FIRING

In a glaze firing, none of the pots should touch each other or be stacked; otherwise they will fuse when the glaze melts. You should allow for the pots to dry off between glazing and firing at least half a day in a warm environment.

Paint a layer of bat wash on the kiln shelves to protect them from drips, runs, and flakes of glaze. Bat wash is a high-alumina mix with some ball clay or china clay to give it a bit of body and help it stick to the shelf. Alumina is a white powder that is inert to heat and provides a useful barrier between the pots and shelf. Bat wash is also available ready-made, and for consistency, I recommend buying it in rather than making it yourself. It only needs to be applied once and can be touched up as needed. If glaze sticks to the bat wash, it can be chiseled off; if it's fired onto the bare shelf, however, it is very difficult to remove.

I recommend keeping strongly colored glazes, particularly ones using chrome or copper, away from lighter-colored glazes during firing, as the color can "leap" through the atmosphere and leach into surrounding pots. This is known as "flashing."

SUGGESTED FIRING PROGRAMS FOR 1,742°F (950°C) BISQUE AND 2,300°F (1,260°C) GLAZE
These programs have two stages, known as ramps, and a hold time called a soak. A soak is a time set for the kiln to even out in temperature and for glazes to mature and become more even or glossy.

Bisque
176°F (80°C) per hour (p/h) > 392°F (200°C), 248°F (120°C) p/h > 1,742°F (950°C), 10-minute soak

Glaze
176°F (80°C) p/h > 392°F (200°C) 248°F (120°C) p/h > 2,300°F (1,260°C) 15-minute soak

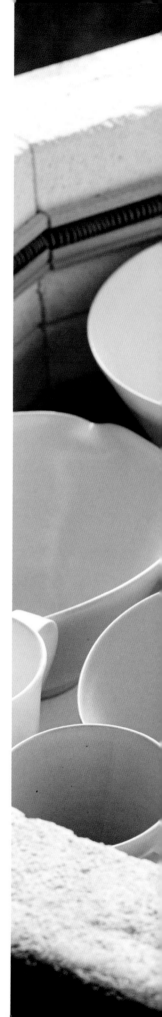

FAULTS AND FLAWS

These diagnostic charts identify many of the common problems that makers come up against when working with clay. The most important step when troubleshooting is recognizing where you are going wrong, so several options for possible causes are listed along with ways to remedy the problem.

HAND BUILDING AND THROWING

PROBLEM	DESCRIPTION	SOLUTION
Clay too wet	Clay is sticky and too soft to work.	Dry out on a plaster bat. If just a little soft, clay can be wedged on a plaster bat.
Clay too dry	Clay is too firm to work easily.	Cut the clay in thin slices, wet each slice, and stack; wrap in plastic overnight and wedge together next day. Prevent drying by keeping clay well-wrapped in plastic or sealed bags.
Air bubbles	There are visible pockets of air, or you feel a soft malleable lump in the clay.	For small air pockets, prick with a pin and work air out before continuing. Revise wedging practices moving forward, as this is the most likely cause.
Mold on/in clay	Black or green mold forms on or in the clay.	Clay has been stored for a long time or has additional organic components (particularly in paper clay) and can grow mold. Most often, this clay can simply be thoroughly wedged and used as normal. In extreme cases, dispose of the clay and use a new batch.
Wedging	You have trouble with air, or the clay feels inconsistent with firm and soft patches.	Revise wedging technique or try a different one (see pages 12–15).
Distorted shape	The form has changed on its own.	See Uneven Drying. Clay may be too soft or have uneven thickness; correct as required.
Collapsing shape	The form collapses during making or afterward.	Consider weight distribution: make the curve even. It should not have too wide of an overhang, belly, or shoulder, particularly when the clay is soft and wet. Ensure wall is thickest at the base and tapers up to its thinnest point at the rim.
Surface cracking	When pinching, fine cracks are spread over the surface or at the rim.	Clay may be too dry, meaning it can't stretch. Hot hands can also dry out the clay—cool them in cold water periodically when hand building.
Uneven walls	Wall thickness is inconsistent.	When hand building, make sure slabs are well-rolled and coils have an even consistency. Work areas carefully and evenly to avoid squeezing a thin patch. With throwing, slow your hands down and lift in an even motion; try to keep a tapered wall, that is thickest at the base.
Handles/spouts crack or fall off	There are obvious defects in attaching areas.	For attaching methods, see Handles, pages 114–119. When scoring and slipping, be sure to score thoroughly and that your slip isn't too wet. One of the most common reasons for this is that the pot is much dryer than the handle, meaning that when the handle shrinks as it dries, it pulls away from the body.
Clay stuck in mold	Clay won't release from its mold.	It's likely that the mold is too wet. Molds are designed to be porous, drying out the clay from underneath and making it shrink and release. When the mold is saturated, the clay will stick to it, as it would to another piece of clay. Allow molds to dry thoroughly between uses and don't wet the clay before putting it in the mold.
Stained molds	The mold has changed color, and this color transfers onto pots.	Plaster molds are porous and can retain color from different clays. This can then be transferred to the next cast. Thoroughly clean and dry the mold between changing clays or, ideally, have a separate mold for each clay color.

DRYING AND BISQUE FIRING

PROBLEM	DESCRIPTION	SOLUTION
Uneven drying	Pots are drying in one area more than another—this may cause warping or cracking.	Often where the pot is thinner, such as at the rim, it will dry more quickly. Pots shrink as they dry and can distort or pull apart in extreme cases. Try to keep the thickness of the walls consistent. Loosely covering with plastic will slow down drying and keep it even. Make sure there isn't a draft around the pot, as this may dry one side more quickly. Again, some loose plastic should help.
Warping	Pots are distorting before firing and become worse in the kiln.	Sadly, this is most often due to poor technique, cutting corners, mishandling, or the careless handling of pieces before firing. Slow the process down and be sure to follow best practices. Also see Uneven Drying (above).
Rim cracks	Cracks form at the rim of the pot during making or drying.	Overstretching clay at the rim will make it split. This is particularly common when throwing. Choose a clay that has more plasticity. Rim cracks also occur when a rim is too thin in comparison with the rest of the pot or when it has been dried too quickly. Avoid drying too quickly.
Spiral cracks	Cracks form around thrown pots at the drying or firing stage.	These cracks are usually caused by pulling up too quickly during centering or centering with dry hands, leading the clay to twist. Heavy throwing rings can also cause this by creating thick and thin areas.
S-cracks	S-shaped cracks form in the base of thrown pots at the bone-dry stage or after bisque firing.	This results from a lack of compression in the early stages of throwing. Try to push the clay down into the base with the broad parts of your fingers rather than cut throughout with the fingertips.
Surface pops	Small blowouts from within the clay or flaky bits on the sides appear; they often have a speck of soft white material inside.	Clay has been infected by a lime-bearing substance. Most commonly, this substance is a fragment of plaster that explodes in the kiln. Check your wedging bats for damage before using them again.
Soft bisque	Bisque is very brittle.	The bisque is underfired or extremely thin. If it is very thin, try to handle with caution; check the bisque temperature with a pyrometric cone—for stoneware, I suggest firing at about 1,742–1,832°F (950–1,000°C).
Explosions	Pots have exploded during firing.	Pots were not completely dry before firing, or the first firing at 392–572°F (200–300°C) was done too quickly. Make sure the ware is fully dry before firing.

GLAZE AND GLAZE FIRING

PROBLEM	DESCRIPTION	SOLUTION
Glaze too thick	Glaze doesn't run off or dry when the pot is dipped.	Add more water to the mix. Water can evaporate if a container of glaze is not sealed properly, and regular use will cause the water content of the glaze to decrease as the pots "drink" it. Do a finger-dip test before every use (see Mixing and Sieving, step 3, page 127).
Glaze too thin	Glaze layer is faded, or pots are saturated.	Allow the glaze to settle and pour out the majority of the water. Mix it up and add water back in until the right consistency is reached.
Uneven glaze	The glaze application is too thick or thin.	The pot isn't being dipped evenly, or the glaze hasn't been mixed properly. Ensure the glaze is completely mixed before applying and re-stir the mixture between dippings. Submerge the whole pot quickly and evenly for 3 seconds only, and remove.
Fingerprints	Colored fingerprints appear during firing.	Fngers can pick up glaze or oxides from the surface of other pieces when moving pots around. Clean your hands after handling pots with different glazes.
Glaze won't stick to bisque	When applying, the glaze runs off the pot and will not adhere.	The bisque is saturated or overfired. Make sure the pot is bone-dry and that the kiln is firing to the right temperature with a pyrometric cone—for stoneware, I suggest temperatures of about 1,742–1,832°F (950–1,000°C).
Brush-on glaze brush sticks	It is impossible to apply the brush-on glaze, as the brush dries out and sticks.	Use a large brush that can hold lots of glaze. The bisque may be too porous, so dampen it down a little with a damp sponge or try bisque firing at a higher temperature.
Dunting	A crack going right through the pot appears during firing.	Heating or cooling too quickly in the kiln, bad design, or poor craftmanship cause dunting. Glaze may have been too thick, only applied on one side, or doesn't fit the clay body properly. Revise making techniques, firing ramps, and glazing.
Crawling	Glaze has pulled away in patches, revealing the clay body.	Make sure the bisque pot is free of dust or grease from fingers. Sometimes, glaze can crawl over underglazes too; if that is the case, re-bisque after applying the colors but before glazing.
Bloating	Large bubbles form within the wall of the pot.	Avoid firing too quickly to ensure time for gases to escape from the pots properly. Avoid wetting the pot once it is already bone-dry.

PROBLEM	DESCRIPTION	SOLUTION
Blistering	Fine bubbling appears on the surface.	This commonly happens from overfiring—reduce the temperature in the kiln.
Transparent glaze is milky	A transparent glaze is coming out milky, slightly opaque, and/or bubbly.	Transparent glaze should normally be applied thinly; it will appear more opaque and white when it is too thick. Underfiring can also cause paleness and a lack of glossiness—try increasing the firing temperature.
Orange-peel surface	The glazed surface is dimpled like that of an orange peel.	Several things can cause this, including firing too fast, bisque firing too low, under- or overfiring after glazing, or spray glazing in dry bobbly layers. See example firing ramps for good speeds; check recipes for ideal firing temperatures; and revise glaze application techniques.
Crazing	The glaze surface has small cracks.	When fine, consistent, and all over, crazings can be a desirable surface effect. It's usually caused by the clay and glaze not "fitting" (having different expansion rates). It can, however, compliment your piece if controlled. If you do not want crazing, you may need to alter the recipe or change clays. If the cracks are large and few in number, it could be that the kiln is cooling too quickly or the glaze is too thick. Don't open the kiln above 392°F (200°C), and even then only open the door slowly over the course of a couple of hours before unloading to prevent thermal shock.
Pinholing	Little pits or "burst bubbles" appear on the glaze surface.	This could be caused by bisque firing at too low of a firing temperature, firing too quickly, or dust on the pot before glazing. Try to eliminate each possibility in order to work out the problem.
Shivering	Glaze appears to be peeling off the pot in patches after firing.	Compressive forces in the glaze prevent bonding with the clay. If you are using a slip under the glaze, it might not be suitable, either. Try revising the glaze recipe, applying the glaze more thinly, or testing different clay bodies.
Flashing	Color jumps from one pot to another due to close proximity in the kiln.	White pots fired beside pots with copper glazes will absorb the green color. Fire white and copper-glaze pots apart in the kiln. Similarly, keep light-colored pots away from dark ones in the kiln.

GLOSSARY

BALL CLAY
Clay of high plasticity, high firing, and pale in color. An ingredient of throwing clay and other clay bodies, as well as glazes.

BANDING WHEEL
A turntable operated by hand, and used to rotate pots when decorating.

BAT
A wooden disk on which pots are thrown, or a plaster block for drying clay.

BAT WASH
Also known as kiln wash. A coating of refractory material applied to kiln furniture to prevent it from sticking during firing.

BISQUE (BISCUIT)
Clayware after the first firing, usually around 1,652–1,832°F (900–1,000°C). Moisture within the clay is driven off slowly in the form of steam, along with other organic compounds. The clay becomes ceramic, a chemical change that is irreversible. Work is often biscuit-fired before being decorated in other ways.

BISQUE FIRING
The first firing of pottery in order to mature the clay and render its form permanent. In a bisque firing, pots may be stacked on or inside each other because there is no glaze to stick them together.

BODY
The term used to describe a particular mixture of clay, such as a stoneware body or porcelain body.

BURNISHING
Compacting a clay surface or slip coating by rubbing a pot in the leather-hard state with a smooth, hard object to create a polished finish.

CERAMIC
Clay that has been fired above 1,022°F (550°C).

CHINA CLAY
A pure, nonplastic primary clay, used in clay bodies and glazes.

CLAY
Naturally occurring material made from weathered granite and feldspathic rock. Primary clays are found where they formed, whereas secondary clays are "transported," perhaps to a river bed, for example. Secondary clays become contaminated with other material, are colored, and, due to the variable presence of fluxes, have a range of lower firing temperatures.

CLAY BODY
The term potters use for a balanced blend of clay, minerals, and other nonplastic ingredients that make up the pottery structure.

COBALT OXIDE/CARBONATE
Powerful blue colorants. Used widely in ancient China, cobalt is said to have been first found in Persia. Blue and white decoration is one of the strongest traditions in ceramics.

COILING
Making pots using coils of clay.

COLLARING
The action of squeezing the walls of a pot in order to draw the shape inward.

CONES
See *pyrometric cones*.

COPPER OXIDE/CARBONATE
Strong colorant in ceramics, creates green to black and brown. In reduction, copper oxide /carbonate can make red.

CRANK
A heavily grogged clay body.

CRAZING
The development of fine cracks which are caused by contraction of a glaze.

DIE PLATE
Usually a square or circular board in wood, metal, or acrylic from which a profile is cut for extrusion.

DIPPING
Applying a glaze by immersion.

EARTHENWARE
Pottery fired to a relatively low temperature. The body remains porous and usually requires a glaze if it is to contain water or food.

EXTRUDER
Also known as a wad box. A manually operated machine for extruding cross sections of clay.

EXTRUSION
A length of clay that has been compressed through a machine and has a cross section determined by the die plate (see above).

FEATHERING
A decorative technique that is used with wet decorating slip. Colors can be layered and pulled through with a feather or other fine tool.

FETTLING
The process of cleaning up pottery with a knife or sponge, especially when removing seams left by a mold.

FIRING
The process by which ceramic ware is heated in a kiln to bring glaze or clay to maturity.

FIRING CYCLE
The gradual raising and lowering of the temperature of a kiln to fire pottery.

FLUX
An ingredient in a glaze or clay that causes it to melt, helps silica to form glaze or glass.

FOOD-SAFE
Pottery or glaze that has been determined to be safe for use with food or drink.

FOOT
The base on which a piece of pottery rests.

FOOT RING
The circle of clay at the base of a pot that raises the form from the surface on which it is standing.

FRIT
Glaze ingredients that have been fused to create a more stable substance and to render any dangerous material harmless.

GLAZE
A thin, glassy layer applied to the surface of pottery.

GLAZE FIT
The extent to which a fired glaze adheres to the clay body.

GLAZE STAIN
Commercial color added to a glaze.

GREENWARE
Unfired clay ware.

GROG
A ceramic material, usually clay, that has been heated to a high temperature before use. Usually added to clay to decrease warping and increase its resistance to thermal shock.

HEAT WORK
The effect of heat and time on a pot during firing.

INLAY
A decorative technique using colored slip. A design is cut into the clay surface and painted over with colored slip. Once firm, the slip is carefully scraped back, leaving only the design filled with the color.

IRON OXIDE
The most common and very versatile coloring oxide, used in many slips and glazes, and often present in clays too. Red iron oxide (rust) is the most usual form, but there are others (black iron, purple iron, yellow ocher).

KAOLIN
China clay. Primary clay in its purest form.

KIDNEYS
See *ribs*.

KILN
The insulated box in which pottery is fired. Kilns can be fueled with wood, oil, gas, or electricity.

KILN FURNITURE
Refractory pieces used to separate and support kiln shelves and pottery during firing.

KNEADING
See *wedging*.

LEATHER-HARD
Clay that is stiff, but still damp. It is hard enough to be handled without distorting a pot's shape, but can still be joined.

MANGANESE DIOXIDE
Coloring oxide produces black, brown, and yellowish tones depending on how thickly you apply it. Will run when applied on or under a gloss glaze. Often used as a decorative edging detail.

MATTE
A soft finish with little or no shine.

MATTING AGENT
Ceramic compound used to create matte surfaces when added to glazes.

MATURING TEMPERATURE
The temperature at which a clay body develops the desirable hardness, or glaze ingredients fuse into the clay body.

MELTING POINT
The temperature at which a clay, in firing, fuses and turns to a molten, glass-like substance.

MOLD
A plaster former in which clay can be pressed or slip be cast to create forms. Molds can be made up of only one section or multiple pieces.

ONCE FIRING
See *raw glazing*.

OPACIFIER
Material used to make a glaze more opaque; often made from tin oxide, titanium oxide, or zirconium silicate.

OPAQUE
Glazes that do not allow other colors to show through, as opposed to transparent glazes.

OXIDATION
Firing pottery in a kiln with sufficient supplies of oxygen.

PLASTER, PLASTER OF PARIS, POTTERS PLASTER
A semi-hydrated calcium sulphate, derived from gypsum by driving off part of its water content. Used in mold-making.

PORCELAIN
Highly vitrified, white clay body with a high kaolin content. Developed and widely used in ancient China, it has low plasticity, which makes it a difficult clay to work with. It can be fired as high as 2,552°F (1,400ºC) and, when thinly formed, the fired body is translucent.

PROFILE
The outside outline of a pot as seen from one side.

PROP
A refractory clay pillar that is used for supporting kiln shelves during firing. Also known as posts.

PULLING
A hand building technique for making handles.

PYROMETER
An instrument for measuring the temperature inside a kiln chamber. Works in conjunction with a probe (thermocouple) placed through a hole that is drilled through the top or side of the kiln wall.

PYROMETRIC CONES
Small pyramids made of ceramic materials that are designed to soften and bend when a particular ratio of temperature and time is reached during firing.

RAW GLAZING
The making, glazing, and firing of pottery in a single operation. Also known as once firing.

REDUCTION
Lack of free oxygen in a kiln atmosphere that causes the reduction of compounds rich in oxygen, which affects the glaze and clay color.

RIBS
Wooden or plastic ribs are tools used to lift the walls of thrown pots, while rubber ribs are used for compacting and smoothing clay surfaces. Some ribs are kidney shaped and may be referred to as kidneys.

SATIN/SEMI-MATTE
A satin-like surface that has a slight sheen.

SGRAFFITO
Cutting or scratching through an outer coating of slip or glaze to expose the different colored body beneath. From the Italian word *graffito*, meaning "to scratch."

SILICA/SILICON DIOXIDE
Primary glass-forming ingredient used in glazes and also present in clay. Silica does not melt until approximately 3,272°F (1,800°C) and must always be used in conjunction with a flux to reduce its melting point to a workable temperature range.

SLAB BUILDING
Making pottery from slabs of clay.

SLIP
Liquid clay.

SLIP TRAILING
Decorating with slips squeezed through a nozzle.

SOAK
Keeping a predetermined temperature at the end of the firing cycle to maintain the level of heat in the kiln to enhance many glaze finishes.

SPONGING
Cleaning the surface of pottery before firing or a decorative method of applying slip or glaze with a sponge.

STAINS
Unfired colors used for decorating pottery or a ceramic pigment used to add color to glazes and clay bodies.

STENCILING
A decorative technique for masking off areas while adding color to the pot. The stencil can be removed, exposing the clay body or a particular color when layering.

STONEWARE
High-firing clay, usually fired to vitrification above 2,192°F (1,200°C).

STONEWARE GLAZE
A glaze that matures within the vitrification range of stoneware clay, usually 2,192–2,394°F (1,200–1,290°C).

THERMOCOUPLE
The temperature probe in a kiln that transmits information to the pyrometer.

THROWING
Clay is placed on a rotating potter's wheel and formed by hand. Most modern wheels are powered by electric motors and come in varying shapes and sizes, but all have the same purpose.

TRANSPARENT
Clear base colors that are free of cloudiness and distortion.

TURNING (TRIMMING)
Trimming thrown pots on the potter's wheel at the leather-hard stage to refine their shape and to create foot rings.

UNDERFIRING
Not firing hot enough, long enough, or both.

UNDERGLAZE
A color that is usually applied to either greenware or bisque-fired pottery, and in most cases is covered with a glaze.

VITRIFICATION POINT
The point at which clay particles fuse together.

VITRIFIED
Usually refers to porcelain and stoneware that is fired at a high temperature. The clay begins to become glass-like and is considered "closed," meaning it will be impermeable to water even without a glaze.

WAD BOX
See *extruder*.

WEDGING
A method of preparing plastic clay by distributing clay particles and additives such as grog evenly through the clay mass. Also used for de-airing and dispersing moisture uniformly through a piece of clay to prepare it for use.

WHEEL HEAD
A circular, revolving, flat disk, attached to the potter's wheel, on which a pot is thrown or formed.

INDEX

ACKNOWLEDGMENTS

There are a few people I'd like to thank—
Quarto for their enthusiasm and belief in me and
this book. The Kiln Rooms for use of the studio as
a location and all of our staff for putting up with
me during this process. The many enthusiastic
and incredibly knowledgeable tutors and mentors
I've had over the years—I hope I do justice with
passing on of the gifts you gave me. My parents,
who were behind me every step of the way on my
journey into the world of clay (even if they didn't
always fully understand it). My wife, Julia. Your
unwavering support and love is a constant
inspiration and keeps me going. I could't do it
without you. Finally, to my son, Leo, you remind
me of the wonder in everything. I want to see
through your eyes and share it all with you.

ABOUT THE AUTHOR

Stuart Carey is a multi-award-winning
ceramicist whose stylish signature
tableware has seen him work with
international clients including Conran,
Calvin Klein, and Goop. Co-owner of The
Kiln Rooms ceramics studios, he regularly
gives talks, demonstrations, and lectures,
and is a contributor to *Ceramic Review* and
Crafts magazines. See more of Stuart's
work at stuartcarey.co.uk.

Conceived, edited, and designed by
Quarto Publishing plc
an imprint of The Quarto Group
6 Blundell Street
London N7 9BH

www.quartoknows.com

QUAR.302744

Senior editor: Kate Burkett
Designer: Jackie Palmer
Photographer: Alun Callender
Art director: Jess Hibbert
Publisher: Samantha Warrington